Building Skills in English

Book 2

A Glencoe Text-Workbook

Consultants

Kim W. Crozier
English Teacher
Lithia Springs Comprehensive High School
Lithia Springs, Georgia

Becky Jones-Calabro
Special Education Teacher
Jerry MacClifton Center
Austin, Texas

Jacqueline Lewis
Resource Teacher
Westlake High School
Austin, Texas

Carol Hance Watson
English Teacher
Harrison High School
Colorado Springs, Colorado

Lynn Marks Wilkinson
Resource Specialist
La Cañada High School
La Cañada, California

Glencoe Publishing Company
Mission Hills, California

D1400658

About the Consultants

Kim W. Crozier is an experienced classroom teacher who has taught a wide variety of language arts courses at the secondary level, including remedial English, drama, and advanced placement English. She received her degree in English from Georgia State University. Miss Crozier is a CVAE English interlocking teacher at Lithia Springs Comprehensive High School in Lithia Springs, Georgia.

Becky Jones-Calabro attended the University of Tulsa, where she earned dual degrees in elementary education and special education. She has taught at the elementary and secondary levels in Oklahoma, Kansas, and Texas. An experienced author, she is working with exceptional students in a vocational training center.

Jacqueline Lewis received a bachelor's degree from Queens College and a master's degree from Stony Brook University. Ms. Lewis earned her special education certification from Long Island University. An experienced author, she is currently a special education resource teacher at Westlake High School in Austin, Texas.

Carol Hance Watson is currently an English teacher and department chairperson at Harrison High School in Colorado Springs, Colorado. She earned a BA in English at Denison University and is an active member of the National Council of Teachers of English and the National Education Association. In addition to her teaching responsibilities, Ms. Watson is involved with various building and district level committees.

Lynn Marks Wilkinson is an experienced elementary classroom teacher and a secondary level special education educator. She received a bachelor's degree in English from Cal State University, Chico, and a master's degree from Cal State University, Fullerton. She is currently teaching special education at La Cañada High School in La Cañada, California.

The Building Skills in English Series

Book 1 • Book 2 • Review Book

Acknowledgments

American Museum of Natural History 83, 84; Leonard Lee Rue III/Animals, Animals 15; The Bettman Archive 6, 21, 35 *top,* 58, 60, 75 *top,* 130; Black Star: Steve Shapiro 50 *top,* John Lapinot 67, NASA 139; Lee Boltin 34; Jane Caminos 9, 17, 26, 31, 32, 38, 45, 53, 57, 61, 62, 63, 65, 77, 82, 88, 105, 109, 113, 117, 125, 129, 130, 133, 134, 141; Culver Pictures 19, 39 *top,* 78, 80, 87, 134; N.P.S./Gamma-Liaison 59; Historical Pictures Service, Chicago 4, 5, 74, 75 *bottom,* 86, 131; Topham/The Image Works 18; Frank Driggs/Magnum 92; Michael Ochs Archives 20; Missouri Historical Society 26; National Archives 122, 123; North Wind Picture Archives 11, 42, 43, 50 *bottom,* 66 *bottom,* 79; Photo courtesy of the National Broadcasting Company, Inc. 109; Photo Researchers: Jen and Des Bartlett 14, Toni Angermayer 30, National Audubon Society 38, NAS 39 *bottom,* 40 *bottom,* Ron Church 102, George Holton 110, Bruce Roberts 135; Stock, Boston: 66 *top,* Peter Vandermark 37, Nicholas Sapieha 106, Peter Menzel 126, Peter Simon 128; Sygma: Sergio Dorantes 27, Randy Taylor 28, 41, 52; U.S. Department of Agriculture 98 *top;* UPI/Bettman Newsphotos 115, 127; Wide World Photos 10, 13 *top,* 20, 54 *top,* 55, 90, 91, 107, 114, 116, 136; Woodfin Camp: © Longview Daily News 1980 by Roger Werth 2

Copyright © 1989 by Glencoe Publishing Company, a division of Macmillan, Inc.

All rights reserved. No part of this book shall be reproduced in any form or by any means, electronic or mechanical, including photocopying, or by any information or retrieval system, without permission from the Publisher.

Send all inquiries to:
Glencoe Publishing Company
15319 Chatsworth Street
P.O. Box 9509
Mission Hills, California 91345

Printed in the United States of America

ISBN 0-02-643342-7 (Student Text-Workbook)
ISBN 0-02-643343-5 (Teacher's Annotated Edition)

1 2 3 4 5 6 7 8 9   92 91 90 89 88

Contents

Common and Proper Nouns

Without Warning

The morning of August 24, 79 A.D., was like most days for the <u>inhabitants</u> of Pompeii (pahm PAY). Wooden-wheeled carts rattled through the narrow streets. Shops were full of busy customers. Some people spoke of the news of the day. Others talked about the games to be held that evening in the <u>stadium</u>. Most of them would never see another day.

Early in the afternoon Mount Vesuvius (vuh SOO vee uhs) blew up. A second <u>eruption</u> was more powerful than the first. Some people ran to the sea. A few of them lived. But most people <u>cowered</u> in their homes and public buildings. Within a day, the city and the people in it were buried. They were covered by 30 to 50 feet of ash and pumice stones.

Building Vocabulary Circle the letter of the word or words in the box below that mean almost the same as the underlined words.

Read the story carefully. Study the words before and after the underlined words. They will help you understand what the underlined words mean.

For more help with finding the meanings of words, see Handbook page 158.

Check your choices in a dictionary. Start a vocabulary notebook with these words and their meanings. Try to use them as often as you can.

1. inhabitants	a. animals b. people who live in a place	c. bad habits d. people who are dead
2. stadium	a. a structure in which games are held b. capsule of medicine	c. motion picture house d. mountain
3. eruption	a. to stop b. lifting	c. part of the ear d. a bursting
4. cowered	a. fearful person b. shaking	c. crouched in fear d. brave person

A **noun** names a person, place, or thing. A **common noun** is the name of a <u>general</u> person, place, or thing. A **proper noun** is the name of a <u>specific</u>, or special, person, place, or thing. Proper nouns always begin with a capital letter.

• <u>Common nouns</u>: man, street, cinema

• <u>Proper nouns</u>: Mr. Harrison, Locust Lane, Cameo Theater

Note that Mr. Harrison, Locust Lane, and Cameo Theater name a specific person, place, and thing.

2

Try It   The words in dark type are nouns. Draw one line under each common noun. Draw two lines under each proper noun. Check your answers on page 4.

1. The **volcano** on **Mount Vesuvius** exploded, throwing **ash** into the **air**.

2. **People** cowered in **houses** and other **buildings**.

3. **Houses** in that **city** on the **Bay of Naples** were set on **fire**.

This is a warm-up exercise. If you make one or more mistakes, read the definitions and examples on page 2 again before working exercise A.

A Identifying Common and Proper Nouns

Circle each common noun in the following sentences. Draw a line under each proper noun. In the first two sentences, all the nouns are printed in dark type.

1. **Heat** from the **volcano** caused **water** to form on the **sides** of **Vesuvius**.

2. The **river** of **mud** swept down on the **town**.

3. In the city, 10,000 people died.

4. The mud that covered the buildings dried as hard as brick.

5. Almost all the inhabitants of the two cities were wiped out.

Sometimes the words a, an, and the come before nouns. Looking for these words will help you identify nouns. Be careful, though. The next word after a, an, or the is not always a noun. Sometimes it is one or more words telling about, or describing, the noun.

B Writing Common and Proper Nouns

Use one of the nouns below to complete each sentence.

soil	**August**	people	**farmers**
world	**tales**	**Vesuvius**	**Pompeii**

1. Today, _____ is the only active volcano in Europe.

2. It is probably the most famous volcano in the _____.

3. It is located in _____, Italy.

4. Vesuvius erupted in the month of _____.

5. Many _____ live on the sides of the mountain.

6. The _____ grow crops in the rich soil there.

7. The _____ at the base of the mountain is good for growing grapes.

8. Old Roman _____ say that the gods used the mountain as a battleground.

Complete the sentences you are sure of first. Mark off the nouns as you use them. Then go back to the sentences you left blank and see if you can find the right noun left in the box.

Number Missed	0	1	2	3	4	5	6	7	8	9	10	11	12	13	14	15	16	17	18	19	20	21	22	23	24
Percent Correct	100	96	92	88	83	79	75	71	67	63	58	54	50	46	42	38	33	29	25	21	17	13	8	4	0

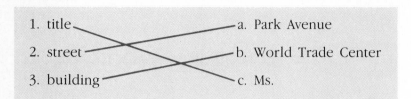

C Matching Common and Proper Nouns

Draw a line from each common noun in the left column to its matching proper noun in the right column. The example in the box shows you how.

1. title ——————— a. Park Avenue
2. street ——————— b. World Trade Center
3. building ——————— c. Ms.

1. river   a. "Star-Spangled Banner"
2. school   b. Canada
3. mountain   c. Mississippi
4. country   d. Mount Hood
5. song   e. Florida State University

Remember, a proper noun names a spe-cific person, place, or thing. Park Ave-nue is the name of a specific street.

D Proofreading

Some proper nouns in the following paragraph do not begin with a capital letter. Cross out the words and write the correct forms above them. The first one is done for you. You should find five more.

                                        Italy
Vesuvius can still be seen in ~~italy~~, but it is not the same as it was long

ago. The height of vesuvius changes each time it erupts. In june of 1900, it

was 4,275 feet high. After the eruption in april of 1906, it was only 3,842 feet

high. Vesuvius is on the mainland of europe. It is still active. Scientists from

the United states and other countries study it to learn more about volcanoes.

Get into the habit of proofreading every-thing you write to correct mistakes.

E Writing Sentences

Write three sentences of your own. Use a proper noun from exercise C in each one.

1. _____

_____

2. _____

_____

3. _____

_____

Try It Answers for page 3

1. volcano, Mount Vesuvius, ash, air
2. People, houses, buildings
3. Houses, city, Bay of Naples, fire

Number Missed	0	1	2	3	4	5	6	7	8	9	10	11	12	13
Percent Correct	100	92	85	77	69	62	54	46	38	31	23	15	8	0

Focus on Writing

Understanding Main Ideas

Paragraphs follow a plan. One sentence, called the **topic sentence**, tells the main idea of the paragraph. All the other sentences give supporting information, or details, about the main idea. Note how the topic sentence in the following paragraph lets the reader know what he or she will learn in the paragraph.

Topic Sentence
The word volcano comes from the Roman god
Supporting Sentences
of fire, Vulcan. The Romans thought that Vulcan

lived beneath an island. They called the island, Volcano.

Each of the following paragraphs is missing its topic sentence. From the list of possible topic sentences, choose the one that best tells the main idea of the paragraph. Write the sentence in the blank.

_____

_____ A volcano begins with melted rock inside the earth. It is very hot deep inside the earth. At 50 to 100 miles beneath the earth's surface, the heat is so great that it melts part of the rock. The melting of the rock makes a gas. The gas-filled melted rock rises toward the surface. As it rises, it melts more rock. The melted rock keeps rising until it forms a pool two or three miles beneath the surface. It stops there until the pressure gets so great that the melted rock shoots out of the volcano.

Possible Topic Sentences

- The gas-filled rock is under great pressure.
- Deep inside the earth it is hot enough to melt rock.
- Most scientists think they know how a volcano begins.
- Eruptions of volcano islands are amazing displays.
- Some people fear the power of a volcano.

_____

_____ The three kinds of material are lava, rock pieces, and gas. Lava is melted rock that has reached the earth's surface. It is red hot. The rock pieces are formed from the melted rock. The gas builds up pressure in the melted rock until it finally blows up. The gas includes all kinds of chemicals. The gas carries dust with it and looks like black smoke.

Possible Topic Sentences

- Volcanic gas is one type of material that is thrown into the air during an eruption.
- Three kinds of material may erupt from a volcano.
- It is not easy to tell when a volcano is about to erupt.
- Scientists divide volcanoes into three main groups.
- As lava from a volcano cools, it hardens into many different shapes.

5

Singular and Plural Nouns

The First Olympic Games

The first Olympic games were held in Olympia, Greece, in 766 B.C. There was only one <u>contest</u>. A cook raced the length of the stadium to win.

Olympic games were held every four years. The games were held for almost 1,200 years. Men came from all over Greece to <u>compete</u>. They ran before crowds of up to 45,000 people. Later, other contests were added.

The Greeks built baths and <u>gymnasiums</u> for the athletes. Later, they built a hippodrome, a round stadium for horse races and other events.

Read the story carefully. Study the words before and after each underlined word. They will help you understand what the underlined word means.

Building Vocabulary   Circle the letter of the word or words in the box below that mean almost the same as the underlined words.

1. <u>contest</u>	a. victory	b. event	c. statement	d. question
2. <u>compete</u>	a. try to win	b. to forget	c. to gather	d. to give up
3. <u>gymnasiums</u>	a. houses	b. walkways	c. streets	d. rooms for indoor sports

Check your choices in a dictionary. Add these words and their meanings to your vocabulary notebook. Try to use them as often as possible.

A **singular** noun names <u>one</u> person, place, or thing. **Plurals** name more than one person, place, or thing. Here are the rules for making plural nouns.

- Most nouns form the plural by adding -**s**: girl—girl**s**, kites—kite**s**.

- Nouns that end in <u>s</u>, <u>sh</u>, <u>ch</u>, <u>x</u>, or <u>z</u> form the plural by adding -**es**: box—box**es**, bunch—bunch**es**.

- Nouns that end in a <u>y</u> that follows any letter except <u>a</u>, <u>e</u>, <u>i</u>, <u>o</u>, or <u>u</u>, change the <u>y</u> to <u>i</u> before adding -**es**: city—cit**ies**, army—arm**ies**.

- Some nouns that end in <u>f</u> simply add -**s** to form the plurals (roof, roofs). Others that end in <u>f</u> or <u>fe</u> change the <u>f</u> to <u>v</u> before adding -**es**: leaf—lea**ves**.

- A few nouns have unusual plurals: child—child**ren**, man—**men**.

- Some nouns have the same form for the singular and plural: deer—deer.

6

Try It The nouns in the following sentences are in dark type. Draw one line under the singular nouns. Draw two lines under the plural nouns. Check your answers on page 8.

1. The first Olympic **record** shows that only one **race** was held that **year**.

2. The **games** were held in the **city** of **Olympia**.

3. In **time**, **events** other than foot **races** were added to the **games**.

This is a warm-up exercise. If you make one or more mistakes, read the definitions and examples on page 6 again before working exercise A.

A Identifying Singular and Plural Nouns

Draw one line under each singular noun in the following sentences. Draw two lines under each plural noun.

Remember that any noun that names one item is singular. Any noun that names more than one item is plural.

1. An event in the early Olympics was the pentathlon (pen TATH luhn).

2. Five contests made up the pentathlon.

3. Each athlete competed in the races, broad jump, javelin, and discus.

4. The javelin and discus are throwing contests.

5. Javelins look like spears and are thrown like spears.

6. Discuses are shaped like plates.

7. Athletes throw them like Frisbees.

8. These contests are still a part of the Olympic games.

9. The Greeks liked the men who were pentathlon athletes.

Most plurals end in s. Watch out for those like children that do not end in s.

B Writing Plural Nouns

Change each singular noun in parentheses into a plural. Write the plural form in the blank space to complete each sentence.

1. There were many Olympic _____. (**event**)

2. In one, two _____ boxed and wrestled. (**contestant**)

3. The _____ did not allow fingers in the eyes. (**judge**)

4. Contestants knocked their _____ out. (**opponent**)

5. Those who did not obey the rules were given _____. (**fine**)

6. Some _____ think the Olympics began as a religious event. (**expert**)

7. Others feel that the games gave _____ practice. (**soldier**)

Refer to the rules on page 6 if you need help.

Number Missed	0	1	2	3	4	5	6	7	8	9	10	11	12	13	14	15	16	17	18	19	20	21	22	23	24	25	26	27	28	29	30	31	32	33
Percent Correct	100	97	94	91	88	85	82	79	76	73	70	67	64	61	58	55	52	48	45	42	39	36	33	30	27	24	21	18	15	12	9	6	3	0

C Writing Plural Nouns — Complete each sentence by writing the plural form of the word in parentheses.

1. Married _____ did not take part in the games.   (**woman**)

2. Unmarried _____ took part in other games.   (**female**)

3. Later, women were allowed to watch the _____.   (**game**)

4. They could even take part in the chariot _____.   (**race**)

5. Greek _____ trained hard for the games.   (**athlete**)

6. _____ in training ate very little in the morning.   (**Man**)

7. Their evening _____ were large, however.   (**meal**)

If you are not sure of the spelling of a plural, try to find that word on pages 6 or 7. If you can't find it, look up the spelling in a dictionary.

D Proofreading — Draw a line through each singular noun in the paragraph that should be plural. Write the correct form above it. The first one is done for you. You should find four more mistakes.

<u>winners</u>
When ~~winner~~ of Olympic contests returned home, the people of their

towns would break a hole in the wall around the town. They were telling all

the Greek that they no longer needed a wall because they had an Olympic

champion to protect them. Poem were written about the winners, and statue

were made of them. group of young people sang about them. The winners

were treated like little gods.

Look for missing capital letters and nouns that should be plural.

E Writing Sentences — Write three sentences of your own. Use the plural form of one of the following nouns in each sentence.

mouse	shelf	fox

1. _____

_____

2. _____

_____

3. _____

_____

Try It Answers for page 7

1. record, race, year
2. games, city, Olympia
3. time, events, races, games

Number Missed	0	1	2	3	4	5	6	7	8	9	10	11	12	13	14
Percent Correct	100	93	86	79	71	64	57	50	43	36	29	21	14	7	0

Focus on Writing

Choosing the Best Topic Sentence

Each paragraph has a topic sentence. The topic sentence, which is usually the first sentence of the paragraph, tells the main idea of the paragraph. For example, the following might be the topic sentence of a paragraph.

> Only two kinds of eagles live and breed in the United States.

A person who reads that sentence will know that the rest of the paragraph will be about two kinds of eagles that live in this country. It will not be about three or more kinds of eagles, eagles that live in Europe, or birds other than eagles.

Each of the following paragraphs is missing its topic sentence. From the list of possible topic sentences, find the one that goes with each paragraph. Write it in the correct blank.

_____

_____

No poems were written about them. No statues were made of them. No one sang of their victories. They were treated poorly by the people of their towns. Members of their own family might even be ashamed of them. For those reasons, no athlete wanted to lose at the Olympics.

_____

_____

The Greeks felt that, by cheating, the athletes had hurt their god Zeus (ZOOS). They were fined for breaking the rules. The money for their fines went to build Zanes, which were statues of Zeus near the stadium. Each Zane had the name of a cheater on it and told how the person had cheated. It was hoped that other athletes would read the Zanes and learn that cheating does not pay.

_____

_____

In 394 A.D. a Greek ruler put a stop to the Olympics. The town of Olympia was damaged by its enemies. Fire and earthquake destroyed some buildings, and others were torn down. A nearby river changed its course and covered the valley with mud. Olympia and its great games were gone.

Possible Topic Sentences

- The early Olympic games came to a sad end almost 1600 years ago.

- Returning home as a cheater was even worse than returning home as a loser.

- Losers of Olympic games did not have a happy life after they returned home.

Possessive Nouns

The Dollar

The dollar is a unit of money used in <u>various</u> countries. Its name comes from the German word *thal*. The word *thal* means "valley" in German. One of the earliest dollars was a coin made in a valley in Germany in 1519. At first, people called the coin by the same name as the valley where it had been made. Later, the coin's name was shortened to *thaler* (TAHL uhr) and <u>translated</u> into English as "dollar." (Notice how much the words "dollar" and "thaler" sound alike.) Both the United States and Canada <u>manufacture</u> dollars. They may be either coins or bills equal in value to 100 cents.

The dollar began to be used in America in 1792. It looked like the Spanish dollar. The Spanish dollar was widely <u>circulated</u> at that time.

Read the story carefully. Study the words before and after each underlined word. They will help you understand what the underlined word means.

Building Vocabulary Circle the letter of the word or words in the box below that mean almost the same as the underlined words.

1. <u>various</u>	a. foreign	c. changeable
	b. special conditions	d. different kinds of
2. <u>translate</u>	a. carry in trucks	c. make in a mint
	b. turn into another language	d. fix the value of
3. <u>manufacture</u>	a. make into a product	c. owner of a company
	b. husband	d. men and women
4. <u>circulate</u>	a. draw a circle	c. become dizzy
	b. go from person to person	d. be desired

Check your choices in a dictionary. Add these words and their meanings to your vocabulary notebook. Try to use them as often as possible.

A **possessive noun** shows ownership. Add <u>'s</u> to form the possessive of <u>singular</u> nouns.

• John**'s** hat, the girl**'s** locker

Also add <u>'s</u> to form the possessive of <u>plural</u> nouns that do not end in **-s**.

• the women**'s** decision, a children**'s** game

If a plural noun already ends in <u>s</u>, simply add ' to form the possessive.

• the trees**'** leaves, the boys**'** lessons

10

Try It

Draw one line under each singular possessive noun in the following sentences. Draw two lines under each plural possessive noun. Check your answers on page 12.

1. Printers' presses were making dollar bills as early as 1775.

2. The mint's first silver dollars appeared in 1794.

3. Liberty's head was on the front of the first U.S. silver dollar.

4. People did not like the coins' heavy weight and wanted paper dollars.

This is a warm-up exercise. If you make two or more mistakes, read the definitions and examples on page 10 again before working exercise A.

Possessive nouns always end in 's or s'.

A Identifying Possessive Nouns

Draw one line under each singular possessive noun in the following sentences. Draw two lines under each plural possessive noun.

1. The new silver dollars' contents have changed.

2. The center's content is now copper.

3. People's interest created a great demand for these new coins.

Hint: Cover the 's or ' with your hand. Ask yourself if the noun is singular or plural.

B Writing Possessive Nouns

Write the plural, the singular possessive, and the plural possessive forms of each of the following nouns.

Singular	Plural	Singular Possessive	Plural Possessive
1. boy	_____	_____	_____
2. puppy	_____	_____	_____
3. coin	_____	_____	_____
4. government	_____	_____	_____
5. glass	_____	_____	_____
6. citizen	_____	_____	_____
7. worker	_____	_____	_____
8. child	_____	_____	_____
9. student	_____	_____	_____
10. jacket	_____	_____	_____
11. house	_____	_____	_____

Number Missed	0	1	2	3	4	5	6	7	8	9	10	11	12	13	14	15	16	17	18	19	20	21	22	23	24
Percent Correct	100	97	94	92	89	86	83	81	78	75	72	69	67	64	61	58	56	53	50	47	44	42	39	36	33

Number Missed	25	26	27	28	29	30	31	32	33	34	35	36
Percent Correct	31	28	25	22	19	17	14	11	8	6	3	0

11

C Using Possessive Nouns

In each sentence, replace the words in parentheses with a group of words that includes a possessive noun. Look at the following example before beginning work.

(**Ideas of the experts**) _____Experts' ideas_____ about the origin of the dollar sign vary.

The group of words you write should mean the same as the group of words in parentheses.

1. Some people feel that the (**S belonging to the dollar sign**)

_____ is a broken 8.

2. (**The mark of that number**) _____ was on old Spanish money called pieces of eight.

3. (**Opinions of other experts**) _____

_____ vary, but some say the dollar sign comes from the Spanish abbreviation for the peso.

D Proofreading

There are six errors in the following paragraph. Draw a line through each error and write the word correctly above it. The first one is done for you.

    coin's
A ~~coins~~ back usually has the words *e pluribus unum* printed on it. That

is the latin motto on the Great Seal of the United States. Translated, it means

"out of many, one," and refers to the making of one nation out of 13 colony.

the selection committees members suggested the motto in 1776. It now ap-

pears on every coin that is minted. Did you know the mottos meaning?

You should find and correct the following errors:
- 2 misspelled possessives
- 2 missing capital letters
- 1 misspelled plural

E Writing Sentences

Write three sentences of your own. Use one of the following possessive nouns in each sentence.

Fred's	students'	reader's

1. _____

_____

2. _____

_____

3. _____

_____

Try It Answers for page 11

1. Printers'
2. mint's
3. Liberty's
4. coins'

Number Missed	0	1	2	3	4	5	6	7	8	9	10	11
Percent Correct	100	91	82	73	64	55	45	36	27	18	9	0

Focus on Writing

Paragraphs and Thinking

Read the following paragraph. As you read it, think about how the writer came to write it.

> Mint marks tell us where American coins were made. A coin with a small <u>D</u> stamped on it was made at the mint in Denver. A coin with a small <u>S</u> comes from the mint in San Francisco. A small <u>P</u> stamped on a coin tells us that it was made at the mint in Philadelphia.

The U.S. Mint

The writer of this paragraph probably noticed that some American coins had tiny letters stamped on them. The person wondered what the letters meant. Once the writer had found out the meaning of the letters, he or she could write the first sentence. This is the topic sentence. The supporting sentences that follow explain the topic sentence to the reader.

Go through the same steps as the writer above. Do the following.
- Look at the pictures of the front and back of the American five-cent coin.
- Read all the supporting sentences in the box carefully.
- Choose the topic sentence that best explains the supporting sentences.
- Write the topic sentence at the top of the lines below.
- Write the supporting sentences in the order they are given.

	Supporting Sentences
	1. On the face of the coin is Thomas Jefferson.
	2. He was the third President of the United States.
	3. Monticello is on the back of the coin.
	4. This was Thomas Jefferson's home in Virginia.
	Possible Topic Sentences
	• A five-cent coin will not buy very much.
	• Thomas Jefferson was an interesting man.
	• There is a bit of history on the five-cent coin.

13

Pronouns

The French Pass Porpoise

It was a stormy morning in 1871. The sailing ship *Brindle* <u>approached</u> French Pass. The captain didn't like using that <u>passage</u> through the islands off the coast of New Zealand. But French Pass was a shortcut between Pelorus (puh LOR uhs) Sound and Tasman Bay. It was well known for its <u>currents</u> and dangerous rocks. Suddenly a porpoise began jumping in front of the ship. It looked as if it were trying to guide it. The ship followed the porpoise safely through the wild waters of the pass.

After that day, the porpoise met every ship and guided it through French Pass. The sailors called the porpoise "Pelorus Jack."

Read the story carefully. Study the words before and after each underlined word. They will help you understand what the underlined word means.

Building Vocabulary Circle the letter of the word or words in the box below that mean almost the same as the underlined words.

1. <u>approached</u>	a. missed	b. fled	c. reverse	d. neared
2. <u>passage</u>	a. go past	b. harbor	c. path or channel	d. rocks
3. <u>current</u>	a. high waves	b. small opening	c. size	d. flow of water

Check your choices in a dictionary. Add these words and their meanings to your vocabulary notebook. Try to use them as often as possible.

A **pronoun** takes the place of a noun. In the following list, the words in parentheses tell what kind of noun the pronoun replaces.

Singular		Plural
I (the speaker)	she (a female)	we (more than one speaker)
you (the listener)	it (a thing)	you (more than one listener)
he (a male)		they (more than one person or thing)

Each pronoun should be placed as close as possible to the word or words it stands for (its antecedent). In the following sentence, the pronoun is printed in dark type, and its antecedent is underlined.

- The porpoise met the <u>ship</u> and guided **it** through the passage.

The antecedent of a pronoun is the word or words the pronoun refers to or stands for.

14

Try It The pronouns in each of the following sentences are printed in dark type. Underline each pronoun's antecedent. Check your answers on page 16.

1. The passage was disliked because **it** was dangerous.

2. The captain decided **he** would take the shortcut.

3. The sailors said **they** wanted to kill the porpoise.

4. The captain's wife said **she** would not let the porpoise be harmed.

This is a warm-up exercise. If you make two or more mistakes, read the definitions and examples on page 14 again before working exercise A.

A Identifying Pronouns and Their Antecedents Circle each pronoun and draw a line under its antecedent. In sentences 1–3, the pronouns are printed in dark type.

1. The captain's wife helped the crew when **she** saved the porpoise.

2. The captain's wife told the sailors, "**You** should not kill that animal."

3. Finally the crew members said, "All right, **we** agree."

4. Most sailors recognized Pelorus Jack when he guided the ship.

5. In 1903 a man was a passenger on the *Penguin* when he shot at Jack.

6. The crew of the *Penguin* said they were sorry that Jack had been hit.

7. Jack disappeared for two weeks, but he later returned.

8. Many sailors said they were pleased that Jack was again guiding ships.

An antecedent comes <u>before the</u> pronoun that stands for it.

B Writing Pronouns Write a pronoun in each blank in the following sentences.

1. Jack would guide most ships, but _____ would no longer guide the *Penguin*.

2. The sailors of the *Penguin* had reason to fear French Pass now that

   _____ did not have Jack to guide them.

3. In 1909 the *Penguin* sailed into French Pass, and _____ did not get through safely.

4. Since you and I knew that Jack would no longer guide the ship,

   _____ guessed that it would be in danger.

5. The *Penguin* struck the rocks in the passage, and _____ broke up on them.

Hint: The antecedent is a clue to the pronoun you should use.

Number Missed	0	1	2	3	4	5	6	7	8	9	10	11	12	13	14	15	16	17	18	19	20	21
Percent Correct	100	95	90	86	81	76	71	67	62	57	52	48	43	38	33	29	24	19	14	10	5	0

15

C Writing the Correct Pronoun

Write the correct pronoun in each blank. All pronouns will not be used. Some may be used more than once.

I	you	he	she	it	we	they

1. Paul and I read about porpoises. _____ learned they are small whales.

2. Mrs. Lerner told us another name for a porpoise. _____ said that a porpoise is also called a dolphin.

3. Dolphins are mammals. _____ have lungs.

4. Tony reported on dolphins. _____ said they are smart animals.

5. Janice talked about porpoises. _____ told us how they looked.

Hint: If in doubt, say the sentence with each pronoun in it. Choose the pronoun that sounds better.

D Proofreading

There are five errors in the following paragraph. Draw a line through each error and write the word correctly above it. The first one is done for you.

They
There are many kinds of dolphins. ~~It~~ range from 4 to 30 feet long.

some weigh as little as 100 pounds. Others weigh 5 tons. Bottlenosed dolphin

live in warm waters. He live within 100 miles of the oceans shore.

You should find and correct the following errors:
- 1 missing capital letter
- 1 incorrect plural
- 1 incorrect pronoun
- 1 incorrect possessive

E Writing Sentences

Write four sentences of your own. Use at least one of the following pronouns in each sentence that you write.

she	he	we	they	it

1. _____

_____

2. _____

_____

3. _____

_____

4. _____

_____

Try It Answers for page 15

1. passage
2. captain
3. sailors
4. wife

Number Missed	0	1	2	3	4	5	6	7	8	9	10	11	12	13
Percent Correct	100	92	85	77	69	62	54	46	38	31	23	15	8	0

Focus on Writing

Working Together

All of the sentences in a paragraph must work together to deliver the paragraph's message. The topic sentence tells the reader what the writer wants to say about the topic. Each of the supporting sentences that follow tells one thing that the writer wants to say about the topic. Supporting sentences that do not belong weaken the writer's message. A writer should always be sure that each supporting sentence tells about the topic sentence.

Practice finding sentences that do not tell about the topic sentence.
- Study the topic sentence.
- Notice that it says two things about the killer whale. It says that the killer whale is <u>both</u> eye-catching <u>and</u> fierce.
- Read the supporting sentences that are listed below.
- Find the four supporting sentences that tell about how the killer whale looks. Put a check mark (✓) in the blank space before each of these sentences.
- Find the three supporting sentences that tell how the killer whale acts. Put a plus mark (+) in the blank space before each of these sentences.
- Find the three supporting sentences that do <u>not</u> talk about how the killer whale looks or acts. Draw a line through each of these sentences.

Topic Sentence

The killer whale is the most eye-catching and fierce member of the dolphin family.

Supporting Sentences

_____ The killer whale may reach a length of 30 feet and a weight of between four and five tons.

_____ The top of the killer whale's body is deep black and its underside pure white.

_____ Killer whales take from 7 to 12 years to become fully grown.

_____ There are two oval patches of white around each eye.

_____ Killer whales can be trained to perform in water shows.

_____ The creature has a high, three-sided fin on its back midway between its head and tail.

_____ The killer whale can swim quickly and knows how to use its 48 razor-sharp teeth.

_____ ~~The killer whale is also called the grompus.~~

_____ It easily catches the seals, birds, and fish that it feeds on.

_____ In herds or packs, the killer whale will attack anything.

Subject and Possessive Pronouns

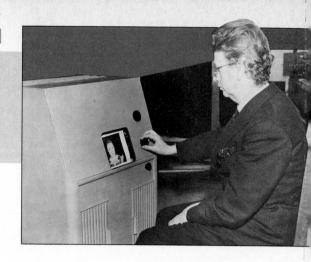

Television Marches On

Television has come a long way since 1925. People saw their first pictures on a television screen that year. The pictures were not very clear. Parts for building a set at home sold in London for $32.

In 1928, General Electric began programming three days a week. Their first show was live on WGY-TV in Schenectady, New York.

Our first regular television broadcasts began in 1931. CBS covered the election of President Franklin D. Roosevelt in 1932. By 1939, television brought us baseball and boxing. The New York World's Fair was also broadcast. A television set with a 12-inch screen cost $625 at that time.

Read the story carefully. Study the words before and after each underlined word. They will also help you understand what the underlined word means.

Building Vocabulary Circle the letter of the word or words in the box below that mean almost the same as the underlined words.

1. television	a. sound sent over wires b. motion pictures	c. system of sending images d. painted pictures
2. programming	a. making a program for b. sending television images	c. watching television d. making motion pictures
3. regular	a. longer than usual b. happening only once	c. shorter than usual d. happening at fixed times
4. election	a. person chosen by votes b. a vote for president	c. choosing by votes d. a place to vote

Check your choices in a dictionary. Add these words and their meanings to your vocabulary notebook. Try to use them as often as possible.

Some pronouns act as the subject in a sentence. They name the person who is doing something in a sentence. These pronouns are in the **subject case**. Subject case pronouns are I, you, he, she, it, we, and they.

- **She** leaves for work at seven o'clock.
- **He** asked for help.

Some pronouns show ownership. These pronouns are in the **possessive case**. Possessive case pronouns are my, mine, your, yours, his, hers, its, our, ours, their, and theirs.

- This is **his** hat.
- The red book is **mine**.

Subject case pronouns act as subjects of a sentence. Possessive case pronouns show ownership.

Try It

The pronouns in the following sentences are in dark type. Circle each pronoun in the subject case. Underline each pronoun in the possessive case. Check your answers on page 20.

1. **I** learned that people first saw color on **their** sets in 1940.

2. **My** television would not be a color set for many years after that time.

3. When did **you** first see a color program on **your** set?

This is a warm-up exercise. If you make one or more mistakes, read the definitions and examples on page 18 again before working exercise A.

A Identifying Subject and Possessive Pronouns

Circle each subject pronoun. Underline each pronoun that shows possession. The pronouns in the first two sentences are printed in dark type.

1. The first television ad on **our** sets cost the advertiser $9.

2. In 1941, **we** saw a program about the United States entering World War II.

3. My uncle says he saw his first World Series on television in 1947.

4. My mother thinks that all sets along with hers were tuned to Ed Sullivan.

5. By 1950 we were watching "What's My Line?" on our set.

If you forget which pronouns act as subjects and which ones show possession, read page 18.

B Writing Pronoun Forms

Fill each blank with a pronoun. Use the words in parentheses as clues. The first one has been done for you.

1. ____I____ (**The person speaking**) have ____your____ (**belonging to you**) set at ____my____ (**I own it**) house.

2. _____ (**My mother**) saw the first "Today" program on _____ (**the set that she owned**).

3. _____ (**You and I**) watched "I Love Lucy" on _____ (**yours and mine**) sets for years.

4. My aunt and uncle said _____ (**my aunt and uncle**) saw the first Academy Awards show on _____ (**belonging to them**) set in 1954.

5. The "Mickey Mouse Club" was seen at many houses, including _____ (**belonging to you**) and _____ (**owned by us**).

6. When _____ (**owned by me**) set was not working, I watched _____ (**the one owned by them**).

Remember that the clues come after, not before, each blank.

'50's T.V. show "The Honeymooners"

Number Missed	0	1	2	3	4	5	6	7	8	9	10	11	12	13	14	15	16	17	18	19	20
Percent Correct	100	95	90	85	80	75	70	65	60	55	50	45	40	35	30	25	20	15	10	5	0

19

C Listing Pronouns by Case

Write each of the following pronouns in the correct column to show whether it is used as a subject (subject case) or shows possession (possessive case).

I	we	it	its	she	he
ours	they	hers	our	you	her
yours	his	theirs	your	mine	my

Subject Case

_____

_____

_____

Possessive Case

_____

_____

_____

Hint: You should find 7 subject pronouns and 11 possessive pronouns. Write 2 or 3 words on each line.

D Proofreading

There are 11 errors in the following paragraph. Draw a line through words that are used incorrectly and write the word correctly above it. The first error is marked for you. You should be able to find ten more errors: six missing capital letters, two incorrect pronouns, one incorrect possessive, and one incorrect plural.

        he
Elvis Presley sang "Hound Dog" when ~~they~~ was on Ed Sullivan's show in 1956. His made $50,000 for being on the program three times. one of televisions longest running shows is "american bandstand." He began in 1957. Other good show of the 1950s were "perry mason" and "cinderella."

Elvis Presley on Ed Sullivan Show

E Writing Sentences

Write four sentences of your own. Use at least one of the possessive pronouns from exercise C in each sentence.

1. _____

_____

2. _____

_____

3. _____

_____

4. _____

_____

Begin each sentence with a capital letter. End each sentence with the correct punctuation mark.

Try It Answers for page 19

1. (I) their
2. My
3. (you) your

Number Missed	0	1	2	3	4	5	6	7	8	9	10	11	12	13	14	15	16	17	18	19	20	21	22	23	24	25	26	27	28	29	30	31	32
Percent Correct	100	97	94	91	88	84	81	78	75	72	69	66	63	59	56	53	50	47	44	41	38	34	31	28	25	22	19	16	13	9	6	3	0

Focus on Writing

In many paragraphs, the topic sentence tells about something that the writer has learned. When someone reads that kind of topic sentence, they usually say, "Why?" For example, We must protect our forest lands. ("Why?") The writer's job is to tell the reader why the writer believes the statement is true.

Tell Me Why

The information given below is the kind of information that a writer needs to write a paragraph that tells why. Complete each of the following steps.

- Read the topic sentence that begins the paragraph.
- Read the four supporting sentences that tell why the topic sentence is true. Number them 1–4 in the correct order. Clues will tell you in which order to number them.
- Read the four example sentences. Identify which example sentence explains each supporting sentence. Number them 1–4 in the same order as the supporting sentences.

Complete the paragraph. Write the supporting sentence that tells the <u>first</u> reason why the topic sentence is true. Then write its example sentence. Do the same with the remaining supporting sentences and examples. The first one is done.

When television first began, few people were interested in buying a set. First of all, the sets were large and ugly. They really looked out of place in any room.	**Supporting Sentences** ____ Finally, there wasn't much to watch. ____ Also, the TV in the late 1930s cost close to $1,000. ____ Secondly, the screens were very tiny. _1_ First of all, the sets were large and ugly. **Example Sentences** _1_ They really looked out of place in any room. ____ This was a lot of money in those days. ____ The first station broadcasted only four hours a day. ____ The first sets had two-inch screens.

Review: Lessons 1–5 Part I ■■■■■■■■■■■■■■■■■■

A Identifying Common and Proper Nouns

Circle each common noun in the following sentences. Draw a line under each proper noun. For help, review page 2.

1. The old man in the gray house on Woodbury Avenue owns three dogs.

2. Many people came to the United States from countries in Europe and Asia.

3. Mr. and Mrs. Wescott have two children who go to Gates School.

4. Dr. White and Ms. Commo come to his office for a test.

5. A good movie is playing at the Acorn Theater.

6. Canada and Mexico are two countries in North America.

7. The World Trade Center is a large building in New York City.

8. Rhode Island is our smallest state.

9. A group of children went on a trip to Mount Rushmore.

10. The Mississippi River enters the Gulf of Mexico at New Orleans.

11. The storm destroyed some trees in Masonville.

12. Ms. Ramos teaches at Winston High School.

13. Two railroads run along the Connecticut River.

14. Did New Mexico become a state in this century?

B Writing Singular and Plural Nouns

Fill in the blanks that follow with a singular or plural noun. For help, review page 6.

Singular Nouns	Plural Nouns	Singular Nouns	Plural Nouns
1. ship	_____	8. _____	cities
2. _____	bushes	9. _____	children
3. story	_____	10. tooth	_____
4. wish	_____	11. teacher	_____
5. woman	_____	12. _____	kitties
6. _____	books	13. _____	men
7. church	_____	14. newspaper	_____

Number Missed	0	1	2	3	4	5	6	7	8	9	10	11	12	13	14	15	16	17	18	19	20	21	22	23	24	25	26	27	28	29	30	31	32	33	34
Percent Correct	100	98	97	95	93	92	90	88	86	85	83	81	80	78	76	75	73	71	69	68	66	64	63	61	59	58	56	54	53	51	49	47	46	44	42

Number Missed	35	36	37	38	39	40	41	42	43	44	45	46	47	48	49	50	51	52	53	54	55	56	57	58	59
Percent Correct	41	39	37	36	34	32	31	29	27	25	24	22	20	19	17	15	14	12	10	8	7	5	3	2	0

22

C Writing
Possessive Nouns

Write a possessive noun that stands for each of the following groups of words. For help, review page 10.

1. belonging to Peter _____

2. owned by the people _____

3. owned by one woman _____

4. owned by more than one man _____

5. owned by more than one boy _____

6. owned by the teacher _____

7. owned by more than one city _____

D Identifying
Pronouns and
Their Antecedents

Circle each pronoun in the following sentences. Draw a line under the word it stands for (its antecedent). For help, review page 14.

1. John saw the bus when it turned the corner.

2. The mother told the children she would be late coming home from work.

3. After the bell rang, the pupils said they were ready to study.

4. Jeanette said, "I read that book last week."

E Identifying
Subjective and
Possessive Pronouns

Circle each subject pronoun in the following sentences. Underline each pronoun that shows possession. For help, review page 18.

1. Did you see their play last week?

2. I hope you know which things are yours and which are mine.

3. We asked Maria if this purse was hers.

4. Ralph said that he read my story.

5. At noon we will have our lunch.

6. This morning she asked if this was your work or theirs.

7. That tree will lose its leaves in the fall.

8. This afternoon I will go to their house or yours.

9. It is a large rock in my back yard.

10. If you do not have a sweater, use mine or theirs.

Number Missed	0	1	2	3	4	5	6	7	8	9	10	11	12	13	14	15	16	17	18	19	20	21	22	23	24
Percent Correct	100	97	95	92	89	86	84	82	79	76	74	71	68	66	63	61	58	55	53	50	47	45	42	39	37

Number Missed	25	26	27	28	29	30	31	32	33	34	35	36	37	38
Percent Correct	34	32	29	26	24	21	18	16	13	11	8	5	3	0

23

A Common and Proper Nouns
Mistakes have been made with capital letters in the sentences below. Find the letter of the mistake. Then blacken the circle of that letter in the answer box to the right.

Answer Box

1. We read Mr. W. Carl greene's book *Now Is the Time of the Brave*.
   a. Mr.   b. greene's   c. book   d. Now

   1. ⓐ ⓑ ⓒ ⓓ

2. Yesterday there was a fire in a building at 1920 Sycamore street.
   a. fire   b. building   c. Sycamore   d. street

   2. ⓐ ⓑ ⓒ ⓓ

3. The Ajax is one of the best Theaters in the city of North Woodlawn.
   a. Ajax   b. Theaters   c. city   d. North

   3. ⓐ ⓑ ⓒ ⓓ

4. My Sister told me that Dr. Small is a friend of Mayor Close.
   a. Sister   b. Dr.   c. friend   d. Mayor

   4. ⓐ ⓑ ⓒ ⓓ

5. Last spring Aunt Millie and uncle Jake went to Paris, France.
   a. spring   b. Aunt   c. uncle   d. Paris

   5. ⓐ ⓑ ⓒ ⓓ

6. My trip from Maine to arizona took four hot, summer days.
   a. My   b. Maine   c. arizona   d. summer

   6. ⓐ ⓑ ⓒ ⓓ

7. Does anyone know the new High school's address?
   a. anyone   b. new   c. High   d. school

   7. ⓐ ⓑ ⓒ ⓓ

B Singular and Plural Nouns
Each of the following sentences has one noun that must be changed from singular to plural or from plural to singular. Find the letter of the mistake. Then blacken the circle of that letter in the answer box to the right.

8. The park has many types of bird, monkeys, and snakes.
   a. park   b. bird   c. monkeys   d. deer

   8. ⓐ ⓑ ⓒ ⓓ

9. The town bought two new truck, a sweeper, and a van.
   a. truck   b. sweeper   c. van   d. town

   9. ⓐ ⓑ ⓒ ⓓ

10. Two boys and three girl started a club at our school.
    a. boys   b. girl   c. club   d. school

    10. ⓐ ⓑ ⓒ ⓓ

11. All the men and woman in our town voted in the last election.
    a. men   b. woman   c. town   d. election

    11. ⓐ ⓑ ⓒ ⓓ

12. It is the hope of every person to have one friends to go places with.
    a. hope   b. person   c. friends   d. places

    12. ⓐ ⓑ ⓒ ⓓ

13. My cousin in Texas wrote a letters inviting me to visit her this summer.
    a. cousin   b. Texas   c. letters   d. summer

    13. ⓐ ⓑ ⓒ ⓓ

14. The boat can hold three men and women or six childs without sinking.
    a. boat   b. men   c. women   d. childs

    14. ⓐ ⓑ ⓒ ⓓ

Number Missed	0	1	2	3	4	5	6	7	8	9	10	11	12	13	14
Percent Correct	100	93	86	79	71	64	57	50	43	36	29	21	14	7	0

C Possessive
Nouns

Find the words that can replace the words in parentheses in each sentence. Find the letter of the words. Then blacken the circle of that letter in the answer box to the right.

Answer Box

1. Mother and Father painted the (**room of more than one child**).
   a. child's room   b. childrens room   c. childs' room   d. children's room

1. ⓐ ⓑ ⓒ ⓓ

2. The (**collar of one dog**) is new.
   a. dog's collar   b. dogs collar   c. dogs' collar   d. dog collar's

2. ⓐ ⓑ ⓒ ⓓ

3. The (**mother of more than one puppy**) fed and cared for them.
   a. puppy's mother   b. puppys mothers   c. puppie's mother   d. puppies' mother

3. ⓐ ⓑ ⓒ ⓓ

D Pronouns and
Antecedents

In each sentence, find the letter of the word or words the underlined pronoun stands for. Then blacken the circle of that letter in the answer box to the right.

4. Three black crows cawed loudly when <u>they</u> flew out of the tree.
   a. black   b. crows   c. they   d. tree

4. ⓐ ⓑ ⓒ ⓓ

5. Nancy, Alicia, and I said that <u>we</u> would always be friends.
   a. Nancy   b. Nancy, Alicia   c. Nancy, Alicia, I   d. friends

5. ⓐ ⓑ ⓒ ⓓ

6. The old man who lives near me said that <u>he</u> had been sick.
   a. old   b. man   c. me   d. sick

6. ⓐ ⓑ ⓒ ⓓ

7. The tall sailor in the torn coat said, "<u>I</u> have been lost at sea."
   a. tall   b. sailor   c. coat   d. sea

7. ⓐ ⓑ ⓒ ⓓ

E Subjective and
Possessive Pronouns

Find the possessive pronoun in each sentence. Find the letter for the pronoun. Then blacken the circle of that letter in the answer box to the right.

8. He and she are going to their house for a party.
   a. He   b. she   c. their   d. house

8. ⓐ ⓑ ⓒ ⓓ

9. Tom and I will follow them to the store in my car.
   a. Tom   b. I   c. them   d. my

9. ⓐ ⓑ ⓒ ⓓ

10. Sam tells me that you are having your room painted by Jack and him.
    a. me   b. you   c. your   d. him

10. ⓐ ⓑ ⓒ ⓓ

11. I was given a dog, but Sarah told me she bought hers.
    a. I   b. me   c. she   d. hers

11. ⓐ ⓑ ⓒ ⓓ

12. She and I will return this book because it is not ours.
    a. She   b. I   c. it   d. ours

12. ⓐ ⓑ ⓒ ⓓ

Number Missed	0	1	2	3	4	5	6	7	8	9	10	11	12
Percent Correct	100	92	83	75	67	58	50	42	33	25	17	8	0

Lesson 6 Part I ■■■■■■■■■■

Regular Verbs

The Big Shake

On December 16, 1811, many <u>residents</u> of New Madrid, Missouri, were <u>flung</u> from bed by the greatest earthquake in history. They raced outside to see the ground <u>heave</u> and the trees tumble. Little did they know that the earthquake was striking a million square miles in six states. It <u>registered</u> 10, the highest possible score on the scale used to measure earthquakes.

On January 23 and February 7, 1812, two more earthquakes rocked the land. Shocks were felt 500 miles away in New Orleans. They were also felt 600 miles away in Detroit. They were even felt in Boston, 1,100 miles away.

How many people lost their lives in the great earthquake? One!

Read the story carefully. Study the words before and after each underlined word. They will help you understand what the underlined word means.

Building Vocabulary Circle the letter of the word or words in the box below that mean almost the same as the underlined words.

1. <u>residents</u>	a. visitors	b. farmers	c. trappers	d. local people
2. <u>flung</u>	a. thrown	b. awakened	c. slipped	d. rolled
3. <u>heave</u>	a. remain	b. ready	c. throw	d. sink
4. <u>registered</u>	a. regular	b. jumped	c. recorded	d. missed out

Check your choices in a dictionary. Add these words and their meanings to your vocabulary notebook. Try to use them as often as possible.

A **verb** is a word that shows action or movement. Verbs tell what people and things do and how they act or change.

• An earthquake <u>causes</u> damage.   • Earthquakes <u>frighten</u> people.

A verb in the **present tense** tells that something is happening now. Present tense verbs end in -**s** or -**es** when the noun is singular, or when the subject pronoun is <u>he</u>, <u>she</u>, or <u>it</u>. Present tense verbs do not end in -**s** when the noun is plural, or when the subject pronoun is <u>I</u>, <u>you</u>, <u>we</u>, or <u>they</u>. A verb in the **past tense** tells about actions that happened in the past. These verbs usually end in -**d** or -**ed**.

Form the past tense of regular verbs by adding -*ed* to present tense verbs that do not end in *e*. If the present tense form ends in *e*, add only -*d*.

Present Tense

The earth <u>heaves</u>.
It <u>scares</u> people.

Past Tense

The earth <u>heaved</u>.
It <u>scared</u> people.

26

Try It   The words in dark type are verbs. Circle each present tense verb. Draw a line under each past tense verb. Check your answers on page 28.

1. Only one person **died** in the earthquakes.

2. We **fear** 50,000 deaths from earthquakes of that size in a city today.

3. We **expect** property damage of more than a billion dollars.

4. In 1811 and 1812, six states **suffered** from those earthquakes.

This is a warm-up exercise. If you make two or more mistakes, read the definitions and examples on page 26 again before working exercise A.

 **A** Identifying Present and Past Tense Verbs   The verbs in the following sentences are in dark type. Circle each present tense verb. Draw a line under each past tense verb.

1. Some trees **cracked** in two during the 1811 earthquake.

2. Windows in some houses **shatter** during earthquakes.

3. Sometimes cracks **form** in the surface of the earth.

4. The Mississippi River and the Ohio River **flowed** backwards.

5. The bottoms of some lakes **lifted** 15 feet.

B Writing Present Tense Verbs   Look at the verb in parentheses at the end of each sentence. Write the correct present tense form to complete each sentence.

1. An earthquake _____ landforms.   (**destroy**)

2. Many earthquakes _____ beneath the sea.   (**start**)

3. In some years, one million earthquakes _____ throughout the world.   (**occur**)

Remember to add *-s* if the word the verb tells about is a singular noun.

 **C** Writing Past Tense Verbs   Look at the verb in parentheses at the end of each sentence. Write the correct past tense form to complete each sentence.

1. About 700 people _____ in the 1906 San Francisco earthquake.   (**die**)

2. Deaths _____ 131 in Anchorage, Alaska, in 1964.   (**total**)

3. The worst earthquake ever _____ throughout China in 1556. (**rumble**)

4. That earthquake _____ 830,000 people.   (**kill**)

Remember to add *-d* or *-ed* to form the past tense.

Number Missed	0	1	2	3	4	5	6	7	8	9	10	11	12
Percent Correct	100	92	83	75	67	58	50	42	33	25	17	8	0

Lesson 6 Part 3 Regular Verbs ■■■■■■■■■■■■■■■■■■■■

D Writing Present and Past Tense Verbs

Write the correct present or past tense verb to fill in each blank space in the following list. The first two have been done for you.

Hint: Remove *-d* or *-ed* for the present tense. Add *-d* or *-ed* for the past tense.

Present	Past		Present	Past
1. talk(s)	talked		7. scare(s)	_____
2. accept(s)	accepted		8. _____	remained
3. _____	acted		9. behave(s)	_____
4. yell(s)	_____		10. _____	dumped
5. _____	directed		11. close(s)	_____
6. soak(s)	_____		12. _____	governed

E Proofreading

There are six errors in the following paragraph. Draw a line through each error and write the correction above it. The first one is done for you. You should find five more.

released
The energy ~~release~~ by an earthquake is huge. It may be 10,000 times greater than that of an atomic bomb. the strength of an earthquake is measure on a machine. Earthquakes sometimes creates great waves. The waves sweeps up on land and are very dangerous. many homes and lives are lost when the waves come ashore.

You should find and correct the following errors:
- 2 missing capital letters
- 3 verbs used incorrectly

F Writing Sentences

Write an answer to each question. Use a past tense verb form in each answer. Use the past tense of the verb in parentheses at the end of each question.

1. What did the earthquake do to the bridge across the river? **(destroy)**

_____

2. What did the earthquake do to the highway pavement? **(crack)**

_____

3. What did the earthquake do to the sides of the tunnel? **(collapse)**

_____

4. What did earthquakes do to lake bottoms? **(lift)**

_____

Begin each sentence with a capital letter. End each sentence with a period.

Try It Answers for page 27

1. died
2. (fear)
3. (expect)
4. suffered

Number Missed	0	1	2	3	4	5	6	7	8	9	10	11	12	13	14	15	16	17	18	19
Percent Correct	100	95	89	84	79	74	68	63	58	53	47	42	37	32	26	21	16	11	5	0

Focus on Writing

Placing the Topic Sentence

The topic sentence is most often the first sentence in a paragraph. When it is, the reader is told first about the writer's main idea. The supporting sentences then tell the reader why the writer wrote the topic sentence.

The topic sentence is sometimes the last sentence in a paragraph. When it is, the writer first gives the reader details that tell about the main idea. The writer then states the main idea that the details support.

Think of a topic sentence for each of the following paragraphs. Write it first or last. Be ready to explain why you think the topic sentence is best first or last. The first paragraph talks about the earthquake that struck Anchorage, Alaska, on March 27, 1964. The second paragraph talks about the damage that took place after the San Francisco earthquake.

Paragraph 1 _____

_____

It was at 5:36 P.M. when it started. Streets burst open. Gaps as wide as 30 feet split the ground. Whole blocks of houses slid about. A brand new six-story apartment house suddenly fell into a heap of destruction. The earth parted under an elementary school and tore the structure to pieces. A quarter-mile section of the main business street was ripped apart. Stores and cars dropped more than 10 feet into a tangle of wreckage. Along the main shopping street of a suburban area, every building taller than one story was splintered. The 68-foot concrete control tower at Anchorage International Air-

port collapsed in a cloud of thick dust. _____

_____

_____

Paragraph 2 _____

_____

On the morning of April 18, 1906, a San Francisco woman struck a match to cook herself some breakfast. There had been a minute-long earthquake in the city four hours before, and she thought that a warm meal would take her mind off the unpleasant experience. The stove's chimney, however, had been damaged in the quake, and her home was suddenly ablaze. Firefighters who responded then discovered that the quake had broken the city's water mains. They stood helplessly by, unable to get at the city's 80 million gallons of water. The fire quickly spread and for the next three days destroyed

hundreds of homes and San Francisco's entire business district. _____

_____

Read each paragraph completely before you try to write the topic sentence. Before you decide where to place the topic sentence, ask yourself where it would best help make the main idea of the paragraph clear to the reader. If the supporting sentences are building towards a conclusion, then the topic sentence should come last. The topic sentence should come first if it will help the reader better understand the supporting sentences that follow.

Future Tense Verbs

Animal Facts

Many people find facts about animals interesting. For example, did you know that <u>reptiles</u> are cold-blooded animals? Their body <u>temperature</u> stays about the same as the temperature of the air, water, or earth around them. To stay alive, they must <u>avoid</u> temperatures that are very high or low. Alligators, crocodiles, lizards, snakes, and turtles are reptiles.

Reptiles come in different sizes. Some lizards are only two inches long. Some snakes grow to 30 feet. Some turtles weigh as much as one ton. Most reptiles are harmless, but some can kill people.

Read the story carefully. Study the words before and after each underlined word. They will help you understand what the underlined word means.

Building Vocabulary Circle the letter of the word or words in the box below that mean almost the same as the underlined words.

1. <u>reptile</u>	a. animal with scaly skin	c. bird
	b. floor or wall covering	d. kind of whale
2. <u>temperature</u>	a. condition of the water	c. strength
	b. degree of hotness	d. appearance
3. <u>avoid</u>	a. like very much	c. draw near to
	b. dislike very much	d. keep away from

Check your choices in a dictionary. Add these words and their meanings to your vocabulary notebook. Try to use them as often as possible.

A verb's tense tells when an action is happening. A verb in the present tense tells about an action that is happening now. A verb in the past tense tells about an action that happened in the past. A **future tense** verb tells about an action that will happen at some time in the future. Future tense verbs are two-word verbs. The future tense is always formed by using the verb **will** with the verb that tells about the action.

Future tense form = <u>will</u> + present tense form without the -s ending. <u>Will</u> is called a helping verb.

Present	Past	Future
Sarah **needs** help.	Sarah **needed** help.	Sarah **will need** help.
John **counts** his change.	John **counted** his change.	John **will count** his change.
The officers **check** the car.	The officers **checked** the car.	The officers **will check** the car.

Try It

Underline each future tense verb in the following sentences. Check your answers on page 32.

1. Flying fish will glide through the air for 1,000 feet.

2. Plover birds will enter a crocodile's mouth.

3. The birds will pick the crocodile's teeth clean.

This is a warm-up exercise. If you make one or more mistakes, read the definitions and examples on page 30 again before working exercise A.

A Identifying Future Tense Verbs

Underline the future tense verb in each of the following sentences.

1. Some whales will weigh 195 tons when they are fully grown.

2. Certain animals will eat four times their weight every day.

3. Will scientists discover more about animals as time goes on?

4. Reptiles will swallow food larger than their bodies.

5. Cobras will attack about 10,000 people in India this year.

6. A baby elephant will grow very little hair during the first year.

7. Some fish will live at a depth of 35,000 feet.

8. I will tell you about ants and other insects.

9. An ant will work hard for its entire life.

10. A mayfly will live for only six hours after it hatches.

Where there's a will, there's a future tense verb form.

Sentence 3 is a question. In a question, the word that the verb tells about comes between will and the verb.

king cobra

B Writing Future Tense Verbs

Look at the verb in parentheses at the end of each sentence. Write the future tense form of the verb to complete each sentence.

1. Reptiles _____ if the temperature around them is too hot or too cold. (**die**)

2. Hawks _____ above a certain spot for hours. (**glide**)

3. Mayfly eggs _____ in three years. (**hatch**)

4. Whales _____ more than 20 feet into the air. (**jump**)

5. An Australian earthworm _____ a length longer than 10 feet. (**reach**)

6. Lizards _____ on black widow·spiders. (**feast**)

7. Some turtles _____ for 190 years. (**live**)

Remember to use will with the form in parentheses.

lizard

Number Missed	0	1	2	3	4	5	6	7	8	9	10	11	12	13	14	15	16	17
Percent Correct	100	94	88	82	76	71	65	59	53	47	41	35	29	24	18	12	6	0

31

Lesson 7 Part 3 Future Tense Verbs ■■■■■■■■■■■■■■■■

C Writing Verb Forms
Fill in the correct present, past, and future forms of the verbs in the blank spaces on the following chart.

Present Tense	Past Tense	Future Tense
1. ache(s)	ached	_____
2. yell(s)	yelled	_____
3. behave(s)	_____	will behave
4. _____	worked	_____
5. _____	_____	will call
6. visit(s)	_____	_____

Hint: Note how the forms that are already filled in were made. Do the easy ones first. See page 26 for the present and past tense forms of verbs.

D Proofreading
Correct the paragraph below. Put in missing punctuation. Cross out any other error and write the correction above it. The first one is done for you. You should find five more.

platypus

       enjoy
You will ~~enjoyed~~ learning about a strange animal from australia Platypus is its name. A platypus has a bill like a duck. It also has webbed feet and lays eggs. Unlike a duck, it is covered with fur rather than feathers. it nurses its young. It uses it bill to scoop up worms and shellfish, and other animals. It will consumed its own weight in worms each day.

Find and correct the following errors:
- 1 missing end mark
- 2 words that should be capitalized
- 1 incorrect verb form
- 1 incorrect pronoun form

E Writing Sentences
Answer each question. Use future tense verbs in each sentence.

1. Will you behave yourself? _____

_____

2. Will Erma call us today? _____

_____

3. Will your cousin visit you this summer? _____

_____

4. Will my feet ache after this hike? _____

_____

Begin each sentence with a capital letter. End each sentence with a period.

Try It Answers for page 31

1. will glide
2. will enter
3. will pick

Number Missed	0	1	2	3	4	5	6	7	8	9	10	11	12	13	14	15	16	17	18
Percent Correct	100	94	89	83	78	72	67	61	56	50	44	39	33	28	22	17	11	6	0

Focus on Writing

Giving Reasons

The topic sentence in a paragraph that gives advice is an **opinion**. An opinion is a statement that may or may not be worth believing. It gives the writer's view of something. To make the opinion worth believing, the writer has to give supporting **reasons** that are **facts**. Facts are statements that can be proved. No one argues with a fact once it is proved.

An opinion is something someone thinks, feels, or believes. It cannot be scientifically proved or measured. For example, what one person thinks is beautiful music might be considered just noise by another. Neither speaker can be proved right or wrong. Each has simply expressed an opinion.

Tell if each of the following statements is a fact or an opinion. Write O for opinion or F for fact. You should find four facts.

_____ Even a "harmless" shark may bite if grabbed.

_____ Sharks are frightening.

_____ Blood attracts sharks.

_____ Noisy splashing attracts sharks.

_____ It may be hard to see a shark at night or in cloudy water.

Follow these steps to write a paragraph that gives advice.
- Write this topic sentence on the first line below: These are good rules to follow to be safe from sharks.
- After the topic sentence, write the first rule in the box below.
- Write the fact from the list above that explains the reason for the rule.
- Write each additional rule and the fact that goes with it.

Rules

(1) Never swim with an open cut.

(2) Never swim at night or in cloudy water.

(3) Swim quietly to shore if you see a shark.

(4) Never grab a shark.

_____

_____

_____

_____

_____

_____

_____

33

Present and Past Participles

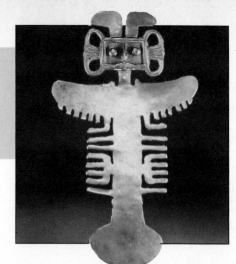

A Lost Treasure

The Spanish came to the New World to search for gold. They found it in the land now called Mexico where it was used for <u>ornaments</u>. The Spanish made slaves of the natives. They also stripped the <u>temples</u> of gold ornaments.

In 1520, the Aztec ruler Montezuma learned that the Spanish were coming. He took all the gold and other valuables from the buildings in his capital and sent them away. The treasure <u>disappeared</u>. Somewhere north of Mexico City a treasure worth more than $10 million may be buried.

Read the story carefully. Study the words before and after each underlined word. They will help you understand what the underlined word means.

Building Vocabulary Circle the letter of the word or words in the box below that mean almost the same as the underlined words.

1. <u>ornaments</u>	a. wristwatches	c. decorations
	b. gold mines	d. important papers
2. <u>temples</u>	a. places of worship	c. places of business
	b. tops of mountains	d. jungle clearings
3. <u>disappeared</u>	a. passed out of sight	c. came into sight
	b. grew larger	d. grew smaller

Check your choices in a dictionary. Add these words and their meanings to your vocabulary notebook. Try to use them as often as possible.

Verbs have four basic parts: the present tense, the past tense, the present participle, and the past participle. The **present participle** is a two-word verb form. It is made by using the helping verbs <u>am</u>, <u>are</u>, <u>is</u>, <u>was</u>, or <u>were</u> with a form of the verb that ends in **-ing**. The **past participle** of a regular verb is also a two-word verb. It is made with the helping verbs <u>have</u>, <u>has</u>, or <u>had</u> plus the past tense form of the verb.

The present participle of both regular and irregular verbs ends in *-ing*. The past participle of regular verbs ends in *-d* or *-ed*. You will learn about the forms of irregular verbs in the next lesson.

Present Tense	Past Tense	Present Participle	Past Participle
slip	slipped	are slipping	has slipped
examine	examined	is examining	had examined
finish	finished	were finishing	have finished
climb	climbed	am climbing	had climbed
hope	hoped	was hoping	has hoped

Try It

The verbs in the following sentences are in dark type. Circle each present participle and its helping verb. Draw a line under each past participle and its helping verb. Check your answers on page 36.

This is a warm-up exercise. If you make one or more mistakes, read the definitions and examples on page 34 again before working exercise A.

1. The natives **were using** gold to make ornaments.

2. The natives **had attended** services in the temple.

3. Montezuma **has stripped** the gold and jewels from the buildings.

A Identifying Present and Past Participles

Circle each present participle and its helping verb. Draw a line under each past participle and its helping verb.

1. We know the natives were carrying the treasure north.

2. Perhaps the natives had buried the treasure in the mountains.

3. People have looked for the treasure in Arizona.

4. Perhaps people are searching for the treasure at this very moment.

5. In 1876, one person said he had discovered a cave with the treasure.

6. Montezuma's treasure is missing to this day.

Montezuma

B Writing Present and Past Participles

Look at the verb in parentheses at the end of each sentence. Use the correct participle form of the verb in the blank space to complete each sentence.

1. In 1914, a prospector had _____ to know where the treasure was buried.   (**claim**)

2. He said he had _____ in a Mexican book to look for markings on rocks.   (**learn**)

3. The prospector was _____ people in Kanab, Utah, to put up money for his search.   (**ask**)

4. In 1922, the prospector returned to Kanab with the news he had _____it.   (**found**)

5. He explained that rocks had _____ a tunnel.   (**block**)

6. Three months passed as the prospector and the people of Kanab were _____ for that sealed tunnel.   (**look**)

Remember that the present participle ends in *-ing*. The past participle ends in *-d* or *-ed*.

Number Missed	0	1	2	3	4	5	6	7	8	9	10	11	12
Percent Correct	100	92	83	75	67	58	50	42	33	25	17	8	0

C Writing Verb Forms

Fill in the blanks in the following chart with the correct verb form.

Present Tense	Past Tense	Present Participle (is, are, was, were)	Past Participle (has, had, have)
1. _____	clapped	clapping	_____
2. _____	_____	touching	_____
3. escape(s)	_____	_____	escaped
4. _____	_____	spelling	_____

Hint: Notice how the verb that is already on the chart is formed. Do the same with the others. Will you add *-d* or *-ed*? Will you have to change y to i before adding *-ed*?

D Proofreading

Correct the following paragraph below. Put in missing punctuation. Cross out any other error and write the correction above it. The first one is done for you. You should find five more.

                                    discovered

The people of Kanab had ~~discover~~ markings on the rocks like those described in the prospectors book They were working on the sealed tunnel day after day. Everybody but the prospector had given up. Finally, he give up too and went back to Mexico to look for more clue. He was never seen again. Do you think the Aztecs had bury the treasure near Kanab, Utah?

Find and correct the following errors:
- 2 incorrect verb forms
- 1 incorrect noun form
- 1 missing end mark
- 1 incorrect possessive noun

E Writing Sentences

Write four sentences of your own. Use a present participle of the verb <u>practice</u> in sentence 1. Use a present participle of the verb <u>look</u> in sentence 2, the past participle of <u>believe</u> in sentence 3, and the past participle of <u>realize</u> in sentence 4.

1. _____

_____

2. _____

_____

3. _____

_____

4. _____

_____

Remember to begin each sentence with a capital letter. Remember to end each sentence with a period.

Try It Answers for page 35

1. (were using)
2. had attended
3. has stripped

Number Missed	0	1	2	3	4	5	6	7	8	9	10	11	12	13	14	15	16	17	18	19
Percent Correct	100	95	89	84	79	74	68	63	58	53	47	42	37	32	26	21	16	11	5	0

Focus on Writing

Writing Explanations

Many paragraphs tell how to do something or explain how something works. Each of the supporting sentences in a paragraph that explains tells about one step. To make the steps easy to follow, they should be arranged in the order in which they happen. That kind of order is called **time order**.

You can help the reader follow the steps in a paragraph that explains. Use words like the following in a paragraph that explains how to do something or tells how something works.

Always keep your readers in mind when you write directions. Use words that are familiar and easy to understand. Make sure your directions are complete. Leaving out a step could leave your reader totally confused.

first	second	third	then	next
begin	start	now	finally	afterwards

Follow these steps to complete a paragraph that explains.
- Write this topic sentence on the first line below: Use a metal detector to find coins, jewelry, and other metal treasures.
- Study the following supporting sentences carefully. They are out of order. The correct order of some steps is given. Supply the rest.

____3____ Plan how to search the whole area.

____1____ Decide where to look for metal.

____6____ Keep searching until you have covered the whole area.

_____ Ask the owner of the land if you can search there.

_____ Take your metal detector to the area and turn on the power.

_____ When the detector shows metal, stop to dig.

- Write the steps from the list in the correct order on the lines under the topic sentence. Use a time word at the beginning of each supporting sentence. The time words will make it easier for a reader to follow the steps.

_____

_____

_____

_____

_____

_____

_____

Irregular Verbs

Outdoor Artist

John James Audubon was born in 1785 on the island of Haiti. His father was a wealthy trader and sea captain. He took young John James to France, because he wanted him to <u>prepare</u> for a <u>career</u> in business. The boy's only interests, however, were painting and the outdoors.

In 1803, John James Audubon moved to Pennsylvania and tried to run a lead mine there. The mine failed, so Audubon moved to Kentucky, where he opened a store. But he failed as a <u>merchant</u>, too. It is <u>fortunate</u> for us that he was not a success at business. Otherwise, he might never have become the country's most famous painter of American birds.

Read the story carefully. Study the words before and after each underlined word. They will help you understand what the underlined word means.

Building Vocabulary Circle the letter of the word or words in the box below that mean almost the same as the underlined words.

1. <u>prepare</u>	a. grow	b. get ready	c. ask	d. lose
2. <u>career</u>	a. ride	b. art class	c. job	d. sail
3. <u>merchant</u>	a. trader	b. soldier	c. engineer	d. contestant
4. <u>fortunate</u>	a. smart	b. quick	c. certain	d. lucky

Check your choices in a dictionary. Add these words and their meanings to your vocabulary notebook. Try to use them as often as possible.

The past tense and past participle of **irregular verbs** do not follow the regular rule of adding -d or -ed. These forms are different and must be remembered. The present, past, and past participle forms of some irregular verbs are shown below.

Remember, the helping verbs <u>have</u>, <u>had</u>, or <u>has</u> are used with the past participle.

For a more complete list of irregular verbs, see page 153 of the Handbook.

Present	Past	Past Participle	Present	Past	Past Participle
begin(s)	began	begun	give(s)	gave	given
bring(s)	brought	brought	go(es)	went	gone
come(s)	came	come	see(s)	saw	seen
do(es)	did	done	speak(s)	spoke	spoken
fall(s)	fell	fallen	take(s)	took	taken
grow(s)	grew	grown	write(s)	wrote	written

Try It

The irregular verbs in the sentences below are in dark type. Draw one line under each past tense form. Draw two lines under each past participle and its helping verb. Check your answers on page 40.

1. Audubon's career as an artist **began** at an early age.

2. As a boy, he had **seen** many birds and animals in the French countryside.

3. Audubon had **done** sketches of the local wildlife.

This is a warm-up exercise. If you make one or more mistakes, read the definitions and examples on page 38 again before working exercise A.

A Identifying Past and Past Participle Verb Forms

Find the irregular verb in each sentence. Draw one line under each past tense form. Draw two lines under each past participle and its helping verb.

Be sure to include the helping verb with the past participle.

1. Audubon gave little time to his businesses.

2. He had fallen in love with the outdoors.

3. In 1819, he had gone bankrupt with hardly a penny to his name.

4. He took a long trip down the Mississippi River in 1821.

5. On this trip, he had seen hundreds of birds for the first time.

6. He brought many sketch books on this journey.

7. At the end of his adventure, he began to paint from his sketches.

B Writing Past Tense and Past Participle Verb Forms

In each blank, write the correct past tense or past participle form of the verb in parentheses.

1. Audubon _____ a search for someone to make books of his paintings.   (**begin**)

2. He _____ to publishers throughout the United States.   (**go**)

3. Those who had _____ his work turned him down.   (**see**)

4. They _____ his art would cost too much to print.   (**know**)

5. In 1826, the painter _____ a trip to London.   (**take**)

6. Within a month, he had _____ to most publishers there. (**speak**)

7. Finally, he _____ to the right publisher.   (**come**)

Check the list on page 38 or on page 153 of the Handbook if you are unsure of the past tense or past participle form of the irregular verbs.

Number Missed	0	1	2	3	4	5	6	7	8	9	10	11	12	13	14
Percent Correct	100	93	86	79	71	64	57	50	43	36	29	21	14	7	0

C Writing Verb Forms

Write the correct form of each verb on the blanks.

If you are unsure of a verb form, look again at the list on page 38 or on page 153 of the Handbook.

Present	Past	Present Participle	Past Participle
1. grow(s)	_____	_____	_____
2. _____	stole	_____	stolen
3. eat(s)	_____	eating	_____
4. _____	rode	_____	_____
5. write(s)	_____	_____	_____
6. _____	took	_____	_____
7. _____	_____	_____	fallen
8. throw(s)	_____	_____	_____

D Proofreading

There are six errors in the paragraph below. Cross out each error. Write the correction above it. The first one has been done for you. You should find five more.

took
It ~~taked~~ 11 years to publish *Birds of America*. During that time, Audubon had wrote five seprate books to go along with the paintings. His books bringed him the money that he never made in business. With it he was able to buy a beautiful home on the Hudson river. It is now called New York Citys Audubon Park.

You should find and correct the following errors:
- 1 misspelled word
- 1 word that should be capitalized
- 1 noun that should be possessive
- 2 incorrect verb forms

E Writing Sentences

Answer each question in a complete sentence. Use at least one past tense or past participle form from exercise C in each answer.

1. How tall did you grow? _____

_____

2. Have you ever fallen down stairs? _____

_____

3. Had the bell rung before the class began? _____

_____

Try It Answers for page 39

1. began
2. had seen
3. had done

Number Missed	0	1	2	3	4	5	6	7	8	9	10	11	12	13	14	15	16	17	18	19	20	21	22	23	24	25	26	27	28	29	30
Percent Correct	100	97	93	90	87	83	80	77	73	70	67	63	60	57	53	50	47	43	40	37	33	30	27	23	20	17	13	10	7	3	0

Focus on Writing

Writing Descriptions

John James Audubon spent hours studying the birds that he painted. Only after close and careful watching could he paint what he had seen.

In writing a paragraph that describes, it is also necessary to arrange the supporting sentences in an order that the reader can easily follow. You might, for example, describe the parts of something from the top to the bottom or from the bottom to the top. You might describe from left to right or from right to left. The important thing is to present the details in such a way that the reader can clearly see what is being described.

Try to use exact and colorful details when writing a descriptive paragraph. Think about how something looks, tastes, sounds, feels, or smells. The more exact and colorful the details, the more exact and enjoyable a picture the reader forms.

Follow these steps to write a paragraph that describes.
- Look at the topic sentence on the first line below.
- Study the picture very carefully from the left to the right and from the bottom to the top. Find details that would make you agree with the topic sentence.
- Write at least six supporting sentences to develop the topic sentence. Be sure that your sentences follow an order that a reader can easily follow. Describe the details that you see from left to right and from bottom to top.

The house was a wreck. _____

_____

_____

_____

_____

_____

_____

_____

The Verb Be

A Big Wheel

Alexandre Eiffel built the famous Eiffel Tower for the 1889 World's Fair in Paris. In 1893 the fair would be held in Chicago. Those in charge wanted something just as underline{attractive} for their visitors. George Washington Gale Ferris had an idea. "Why not build the world's largest wheel?" he asked. The wheel was built as planned. It was 250 feet in diameter. It was held off the ground by two 140-foot towers. Cars attached to the wheel were 24 feet long, 13 feet wide, and 10 feet high. Each of the 36 cars could carry up to 60 passengers. It took two 1,000-horsepower steam engines to turn the wheel. Today, smaller wheels like this are called Ferris wheels.

Read the story carefully. Study the words before and after each underlined word. They will help you understand what the underlined word means.

Building Vocabulary   Circle the letter of the word or words in the box below that mean almost the same as the underlined words.

1. attractive	a. big	b. tall	c. expensive	d. charming
2. diameter	a. total weight	b. put in place	c. length through the center	d. placed on its side
3. attached	a. given	b. came up	c. fastened to	d. stretched

Check your choices in a dictionary. Add these words and their meanings to your vocabulary notebook. Try to use them as often as possible.

The verb be is a very important verb that we use all the time. It has different forms for the different tenses. All of the forms of be are irregular. Here are the present and past forms.

Remember, the forms of be are all irregular. They should be memorized.

Present Tense		Past Tense	
singular (1)	**plural (2+)**	**singular (1)**	**plural (2+)**
I am	we are	I was	we were
you are	you are	you were	you were
he, she, it is	they are	he, she, it was	they were

The present participle of be is being. The past participle is been: The baby **is being** stubborn. The baby **has been** good.

With the participle forms, the helping verb changes to agree with the subject. Remember to use has, have, or had with past participles.

Form the future tense by using will with be: I **will be** home this evening.

Try It
Underline the forms of the verb be in the following sentences. Check your answers on page 44.

1. A Ferris wheel is an interesting ride.

2. Most modern Ferris wheels are smaller than the original one.

3. Two of them were here at our local amusement park.

This is a warm-up exercise. If you make one or more mistakes, read the definitions and examples on page 42 again before working exercise A.

A Identifying Forms of Be

A form of be in each sentence is printed in dark type. In the spaces after the sentences, identify each form of the verb be by writing present, past, present participle, past participle, or future.

1. The Eiffel Tower **is** in Paris. _____

2. The Eiffel Tower **is** 1,052 feet high. _____

3. The first Ferris wheel **was** the largest wheel in the world at that time.

_____

4. There **had been** a smaller wheel on the Isle of Man. _____

5. The first Ferris wheel **was** more than three times larger than the Isle of

Man wheel. _____

6. Many people **have been** on Ferris wheels since 1893. _____

7. I **am** a person who likes to ride on Ferris wheels. _____

8. The one-hundredth anniversary of the Ferris wheel **will be** in 1993.

_____

For help in identifying the tenses of be, see the chart on page 42.

B Writing Forms of Be

Complete each sentence with one of the forms of the verb be in parentheses.

1. Building the first Ferris wheel _____ a big job.   (**is, was**)

2. The wheel _____ almost as wide as a football field.   (**was, were**)

3. Mr. Ferris had _____ a bridge engineer.   (**be, been**)

4. The wheel's axle _____ 45½ feet long.   (**was, were**)

5. It _____ then the largest single piece of steel ever made in this country.   (**was, were**)

If in doubt, say the sentence with each verb in the blank. Choose the form you think sounds best.

Number Missed	0	1	2	3	4	5	6	7	8	9	10	11	12	13
Percent Correct	100	92	85	77	69	62	54	46	38	31	23	15	8	0

C Writing Forms of Be   Use one of the forms of be in the box to complete each sentence.

been	being	were	be	was

1. Yesterday I _____ at the amusement park.

2. My friends and I _____ the only ones on the roller coaster.

3. I had _____ there a week before, too.

4. All the workers at the park were _____ very helpful to us.

5. I will _____ back at the park again next week.

Use each verb in the box once. Do the easy ones first.

D Proofreading   Correct the paragraph below. Add the missing end mark. Cross out every other error. Write the correction above it. The first one is marked for you. You should find five more.

                                  seen
Until 1893, people had never ~~saw~~ such a large wheel. They enjoy their ride on it. Newspapers wrote about the wheel. It drew many people to the Worlds Fair that year. Many people had rode on the wheel by the end of the year The cars he rode on weighed 13 tons. Later, a larger wheel was built, but people remembered that first wheel.

Find and correct the following errors:
- **2 incorrect verb forms**
- **1 missing end mark**
- **1 incorrect pronoun form**
- **1 incorrect possessive noun**

E Writing Sentences   Write four sentences of your own about yourself. Follow the directions for each sentence.

1. Use the future tense of the verb be: _____

2. Use the present participle of be with was: _____

3. Use the past participle of be with has: _____

4. Use the past tense of be: _____

Try It Answers for page 43

1. is
2. are
3. were

Number Missed	0	1	2	3	4	5	6	7	8	9	10	11	12	13	14
Percent Correct	100	93	86	79	71	64	57	50	43	36	29	21	14	7	0

Focus on Writing

Telling What Happened

Paragraphs that tell what happened are called **narrative** paragraphs. A narrative is a telling of events. The writer must be sure that the reader understands the order in which the events took place.

In some narrative paragraphs, there is no topic sentence. The writer simply tells about the other events in the order in which they took place. Many narrative paragraphs, however, do have a topic sentence. The topic sentence might tell why the events were important, or what the events mean.

Narrative paragraphs are like stories. They may tell about a personal experience you have had or something that happened to someone you know. It is good to begin a narrative paragraph with a sentence that grabs the reader's interest.

Do the following. Complete each step before going on to the one that follows.
• Study the topic sentence and the list of supporting sentences.
• Decide which of the sentences should come right after the topic sentence. Write the number 1 in the space before it.
• Decide the order of the sentences that remain. In the space before each, write a number from 2 to 8.
• Complete the paragraph by writing the supporting sentences in the correct time order.

The Ferris wheel turned my sister Emily into an amusement park daredevil. _____	**Supporting Sentences**
	____ When the wheel reached the top, she said, "This is great!"
	____ When the day finally came, we took the bus to the park.
	____ She bravely told me the Ferris wheel was her choice.
	____ We planned our amusement park trip two weeks in advance, but I could tell Emily was not anxious to go.
	____ I began to regret that I had brought her to the park when she took me to a ride called "Plunge Through Space."
	____ Once aboard, the wheel began to turn. Emily was nervous.
	____ As soon as we entered the park, I asked Emily what ride she wanted to try first.
	____ When the Ferris wheel ride ended, she told me to follow her.

Review: Lessons 6–10 Part 1 ■■■■■■■■■■■■■■■■■

A Identifying Regular Present and Past Tense Verbs

Circle each present tense verb in the following sentences. Draw a line under each past tense verb. For help, review page 26.

1. The clerk added fifty cents to the bill for tax.

2. The young boy yelled for help.

3. Most people admire students with good grades.

4. She touched the tea kettle on the hot stove.

5. Father tossed the newspaper on the table.

6. This car needs a lot of repair work.

7. Gail studies for two hours every night.

8. The coach helped the new players.

9. That radio sounds fine.

10. We want new uniforms for our team.

B Writing Future Tense Verbs

Complete each sentence with the future tense of the verb in parentheses. For help, review page 30.

1. I _____ you sometime during the week.   (**call**)

2. Catch the cat or it _____ on the table.   (**leap**)

3. If you sit on that hat you _____ it.   (**crush**)

4. I _____ lunch with my friends at noon.   (**eat**)

5. The artist _____ a picture of the sunset.   (**paint**)

C Writing Present and Past Participles

Complete each sentence with the correct form of the verb in parentheses. For help, review page 34.

1. They were _____ for her purse.   (**search**)

2. He had _____ before eight o'clock.   (**return**)

3. We have _____ that mountain six times.   (**climb**)

4. My friend is _____ to swim.   (**learn**)

5. The stove has _____ to keep us warm all winter.   (**fail**)

Number Missed	0	1	2	3	4	5	6	7	8	9	10	11	12	13	14	15	16	17	18	19	20
Percent Correct	100	95	90	85	80	75	70	65	60	55	50	45	40	35	30	25	20	15	10	5	0

46

D Writing
Irregular Verb
Forms

Complete the following chart by writing the correct form of
the verb in each blank. For help, review page 38.

Present	Past	Present Participle (is, are, was, were)	Past Participle (has, had, have)
1. begin(s)	_____	beginning	begun
2. write(s)	wrote	_____	_____
3. break(s)	_____	_____	broken
4. know(s)	_____	_____	_____
5. _____	_____	riding	_____
6. _____	_____	_____	brought
7. _____	came	_____	_____
8. do(es)	_____	_____	_____
9. _____	_____	giving	_____
10. eat(s)	_____	_____	_____
11. _____	_____	falling	_____
12. _____	went	_____	_____
13. run(s)	_____	_____	_____
14. see(s)	_____	_____	_____

E Using Forms
of Be

Complete each sentence with one of the verbs in parentheses. For help, review page 42.

1. I hate it when I (**am, is**) _____ late for work.

2. Those two girls (**is, are**) _____ sisters.

3. All week long I have (**be, been**) _____ happy.

4. Thank you for (**be, being**) _____ so kind to my friends.

5. Yesterday (**was, were**) _____ the last day of the month.

Number Missed	0	1	2	3	4	5	6	7	8	9	10	11	12	13	14	15	16	17	18	19	20	21	22	23	24	25	26	27	28	29	30	31	32	33	34
Percent Correct	100	98	95	93	91	88	86	84	81	79	77	74	72	70	67	65	63	60	58	56	53	51	49	47	44	42	40	37	35	33	30	28	26	23	21

Number Missed	35	36	37	38	39	40	41	42	43
Percent Correct	19	16	14	12	9	7	5	2	0

A Past Tense Verbs

Find the letter of the past tense verb that will correctly complete each of the following sentences. Then blacken the circle of that letter in the answer box to the right.

Answer Box

1. The smaller children _____ at the park.

   a. stay   b. will stay   c. stayed   d. is staying

   1. ⓐ ⓑ ⓒ ⓓ

2. The little kitten _____ very quickly.

   a. growed   b. grew   c. grown   d. grows

   2. ⓐ ⓑ ⓒ ⓓ

3. My father _____ a train to Detroit.

   a. took   b. takes   c. taken   d. taked

   3. ⓐ ⓑ ⓒ ⓓ

4. I _____ my bicycle around the track.

   a. rided   b. rode   c. ridden   d. rides

   4. ⓐ ⓑ ⓒ ⓓ

B Future Tense Verbs

Find the letter of the word or words that are the future tense verb in each sentence. Then blacken the circle of that letter in the answer box to the right.

5. I will talk to the class about my trip to South Dakota last year.

   a. will   b. talk   c. will talk   d. last year

   5. ⓐ ⓑ ⓒ ⓓ

6. My aunt and uncle will grow tomatoes and corn in their garden this summer.

   a. aunt   uncle   b. will grow   c. tomatoes   corn   d. their garden

   6. ⓐ ⓑ ⓒ ⓓ

7. At camp my brother will make a leather necklace for me.

   a. camp   b. my brother   c. will make   d. leather

   7. ⓐ ⓑ ⓒ ⓓ

8. Some cats will live to be 20 years old.

   a. Some   b. Some cats   c. will live   d. years

   8. ⓐ ⓑ ⓒ ⓓ

C Present Participles

Choose the present participle form that correctly completes each of the following sentences. Then blacken the circle of that letter in the answer box to the right.

9. My mother is _____ in the city now.

   a. work   b. worked   c. working   d. works

   9. ⓐ ⓑ ⓒ ⓓ

10. I was _____ to Mr. Irwin yesterday.

   a. spoken   b. spoked   c. speaking   d. spoke

   10. ⓐ ⓑ ⓒ ⓓ

11. They were _____ toward the finish line.

   a. runned   b. running   c. run   d. ran

   11. ⓐ ⓑ ⓒ ⓓ

12. A large branch is _____ over the street.

   a. hanged   b. hung   c. hang   d. hanging

   12. ⓐ ⓑ ⓒ ⓓ

Number Missed	0	1	2	3	4	5	6	7	8	9	10	11	12
Percent Correct	100	92	83	75	67	58	50	42	33	25	17	8	0

D Past Participles

Choose the past participle form that correctly completes each of the following sentences. Then blacken the circle of that letter in the answer box to the right.

Answer Box

1. I have _____ a four-page report.
   a. writing   b. written   c. writed   d. wrote
   1. ⓐ ⓑ ⓒ ⓓ

2. If I had _____ Jackie last Saturday, I would have invited her.
   a. seen   b. saw   c. seed   d. seeing
   2. ⓐ ⓑ ⓒ ⓓ

3. Tony had _____ on the slippery sidewalk twice before.
   a. fell   b. fallen   c. fall   d. falled
   3. ⓐ ⓑ ⓒ ⓓ

4. Our track team has _____ the school record.
   a. broken   b. breaked   c. brake   d. break
   4. ⓐ ⓑ ⓒ ⓓ

5. We have _____ these photographs for many years.
   a. save   b. saven   c. saved   d. saves
   5. ⓐ ⓑ ⓒ ⓓ

6. My cousin has _____ in five races.
   a. ran   b. run   c. runs   d. runned
   6. ⓐ ⓑ ⓒ ⓓ

7. We have _____ all the trash into this bag.
   a. throwed   b. throw   c. threw   d. thrown
   7. ⓐ ⓑ ⓒ ⓓ

E Forms of Be

Choose the form of be that correctly completes each of the following sentences. Then blacken the circle of that letter in the answer box to the right.

8. My brother will _____ 16 years old next month.
   a. being   b. are   c. be   d. been
   8. ⓐ ⓑ ⓒ ⓓ

9. Both cats _____ on the sofa.
   a. was   b. is   c. were   d. being
   9. ⓐ ⓑ ⓒ ⓓ

10. Mai _____ the best player on our team.
    a. were   b. being   c. was   d. been
    10. ⓐ ⓑ ⓒ ⓓ

11. The new jacket _____ on the floor.
    a. were   b. am   c. was   d. were
    11. ⓐ ⓑ ⓒ ⓓ

12. I _____ the new secretary of the club.
    a. is   b. are   c. be   d. am
    12. ⓐ ⓑ ⓒ ⓓ

13. We have _____ here for three hours.
    a. be   b. being   c. been   d. is
    13. ⓐ ⓑ ⓒ ⓓ

14. The mistakes _____ ours.
    a. was   b. been   c. were   d. being
    14. ⓐ ⓑ ⓒ ⓓ

Number Missed	0	1	2	3	4	5	6	7	8	9	10	11	12	13	14
Percent Correct	100	93	86	79	71	64	57	50	43	36	29	21	14	7	0

Object Pronouns

The Big Wave

It was afternoon in Galveston (GAL vuh stuhn), Texas. The date was September 8, 1900. All day long the residents of Galveston had watched the storm grow stronger. Joseph Cline, a worker for the weather bureau (BYOOR·oh), climbed to the top of the Levi Building. He looked down and saw that half the city was under water.

People began to leave the city. Galveston is on an island two miles off the Texas coast. It was already too late to get to the mainland.

At 7:32 P.M. a tidal wave, caused by the hurricane, struck. It threw large ships into the city and smashed houses. It resulted in 17 million dollars in property damage and left 6,000 people dead.

Read the story carefully. Study the words before and after each underlined word. They will help you understand what the underlined word means.

Building Vocabulary Circle the letter of the word or words in the box below that mean almost the same as the underlined words.

1. residents	a. leftovers	b. bad storms	c. news reporters	d. people who live in a place
2. bureau	a. house	b. department	c. forecast	d. balloon
3. mainland	a. island	b. beach	c. major land mass	d. suburbs
4. property	a. cities	b. possessions	c. terrible	d. money

Check your choices in a dictionary. Add these words and their meanings to your vocabulary notebook. Try to use them as often as possible.

Remember, a **pronoun** is a word that takes the place of a noun. Some pronouns tell who or what did something:

• **He** works for Mr. White.

Other pronouns tell who or what receives the action of the verb:

• Mr. White pays **him** well.

Pronouns that receive the action of the verb are called **object pronouns**. The object forms of pronouns are listed below.

me	you	him	her	it	us	them

Try It

Underline each object pronoun in the following sentences. Check your answers on page 52.

1. When the storm started, people did not see it as a problem.

2. They were not alarmed when they first felt the rain strike them.

3. Would the warning have given us time to get to the mainland?

This is a warm-up exercise. If you make one or more mistakes, read the definitions and examples on page 50 again before working exercise A.

A Identifying Object Pronouns

Underline each object pronoun in the following sentences. There is an object pronoun in each sentence.

1. The people of Galveston lived near the sea and loved it.

2. The storm did not frighten them at first.

3. The wind, which Anna usually loved, pushed her roughly down the street.

4. The darkening sky frightened us.

5. A reporter told me that soon most people were safely inside buildings.

B Writing Object Pronouns

Choose one of the words in parentheses to complete each sentence correctly. Write your choices in the blank spaces.

1. History tells _____ that people lived on Galveston Island in 1836.   (**we, us**)

2. Bad storms did not bother _____ in those early years. (**they, them**)

3. Richard Spillane, a newspaper editor, said the storm terrified

   _____.   (**he, him**)

4. People in houses were afraid to leave _____.   (**they, them**)

5. A little girl screamed when the wind blew _____ off her feet. (**she, her**)

6. As I told _____, the storm was a hurricane.   (**you, your**)

7. It strikes _____ that a hurricane is dangerous.   (**I, me**)

8. I hope that one does not hit _____ this year.   (**we, us**)

9. If there is a hurricane coming, the weather bureau will warn you and

   _____.   (**I, me**)

Try out each word. Choose the one that sounds right.

Number Missed	0	1	2	3	4	5	6	7	8	9	10	11	12	13	14
Percent Correct	100	93	86	79	71	64	57	50	43	36	29	21	14	7	0

51

C Using Object Pronouns

Complete each sentence. Write an object pronoun on the line instead of the words in parentheses.

1. Water flooded the streets and covered (**the streets**) _____.

2. Some people waded out of the city and left (**the city**) _____.

3. Records tell (**you and me**) _____ when the tidal wave struck.

4. One woman was saved when two nuns caught (**the woman**) _____ as she swept past their building.

5. One man died when his roof fell and crushed (**the man**) _____.

Check the list of object pronouns on page 50. Choose the form that makes sense in each sentence.

D Proofreading

Correct each error. Cross out the error and write the correction above it. There are six errors. The first error is marked. You should find and correct five more.

    The city went dark when the power plant failed and left ~~her~~ *it* without light. Some people waded to higher ground, thinking the height would save they. Then the tidal wave struck. all the animals at the shelter on slater Avenue were drowned. One house was destroy by a large section of railroad track. More than 50 people was in the house, trying to escape from the storm.

You should find and correct the following errors:
- 1 incorrect pronoun forms
- 2 incorrect verb forms
- 2 words that need to be capitalized

E Writing Sentences

Write four sentences of your own that tell about the worst storm you have ever experienced. In each sentence, use at least one of the object pronouns shown on page 50.

1. _____

   _____

2. _____

   _____

3. _____

   _____

4. _____

   _____

Remember to begin each sentence with a capital letter. End each sentence with the correct punctuation mark.

Try It Answers for page 51

1. it
2. them
3. us

Number Missed	0	1	2	3	4	5	6	7	8	9	10	11	12	13	14
Percent Correct	100	93	86	79	71	64	57	50	43	36	29	21	14	7	0

Focus on Writing

Writing a Friendly Letter

A **friendly letter** is one that you would write to a member of your family or a friend. A friendly letter has five parts. These five parts are labeled in the letter below.

(Heading) 128 Fallen Leaf Lane
Sale City, GA 31784
October 6, 1989

Dear Herb,   **(Greeting)**

A lot has happened since I last wrote.

The hurricane that moved up the coast hit here. There are   **(Body)**
badly damaged houses all round us, and the downtown area is a
mess. The winds began to howl yesterday afternoon and didn't
die down for five hours. Wires are down everywhere, and no one
has electricity. There are trees down all along this street.

Please write and tell me if the storm was felt in your area.

(Closing) Your friend,

(Signature) *Steve*

Note the use of capital letters and commas in the heading, the greeting, and the closing of the letter.

Your letter should be at least three paragraphs long. In the first paragraph, tell briefly about what you have been doing lately. In the second, tell about your experience or make a suggestion for a future activity that you could both do. In the third, ask your friend to write back to you.

Write a friendly letter. Follow these steps.
- Write your own address and today's date in the heading.
- Write the name of a friend in the greeting.
- In the body of the letter, tell about an interesting experience you had recently. Include something that will make the reader want to write back to you.
- Use whatever closing you wish and sign your name.

Adjectives

The Greatest Baseball Team

In 1970 NBC decided to find out which was the best baseball team since 1920. They picked the 1951 New York Giants and the 1969 New York Mets. Then they asked baseball fans for their choices. They took the top six teams. Three of the top six teams were the 1927 New York Yankees, the 1929 Philadelphia Athletics, and the 1955 Brooklyn Dodgers. Also picked were the 1942 St. Louis Cardinals, the 1961 New York Yankees, and the 1963 Los Angeles Dodgers.

NBC then fed the records of the eight teams into a <u>computer</u>. They had them play a <u>series</u>. The winners of the first four games met in two <u>semifinal</u> games. Those winners played the big <u>championship</u> game. In the final game, the 1927 Yankees beat the 1961 Yankees by a score of 5–3.

> Read the story carefully. Study the words before and after each underlined word. They will help you understand what the underlined word means.

Building Vocabulary Circle the letter of the word or words in the box below that mean almost the same as the underlined words.

1. <u>computer</u>	a. file cabinet b. drawer	c. problem-solving machine d. arithmetic book
2. <u>series</u>	a. an important game b. events in a row	c. baseball players d. not funny
3. <u>semifinal</u>	a. next-to-last game b. the last game	c. game not played d. winning game
4. <u>championship</u>	a. home of a champion b. boat of a champion	c. story of a winner d. game that decides the winner

> Check your choices in a dictionary. Add these words and their meanings to your vocabulary notebook. Try to use them as often as possible.

An **adjective** is a word that modifies, or describes, a noun or pronoun. An adjective may tell what kind, how many, or which one.

* **warm** day; **long** trip (what kind)

* **23** dogs; **many** men (how many)

* **this** book; **those** apples (which one)

Try It
Underline the noun that each adjective in dark type modifies. Check your answers on page 56.

1. Fans picked the **best** teams.

2. **Many** players were no longer playing.

3. NBC had a **hard** time picking the winner.

This is a warm-up exercise. If you make one or more mistakes, read the definitions and examples on page 54 again before working exercise A.

A Identifying Adjectives and the Words They Modify

Underline the noun that each adjective in dark type modifies.

1. NBC was not able to use **all** teams in the series.

2. Nine teams not chosen for the series were **excellent** teams.

3. The records of the teams were fed into a **powerful** computer.

4. Babe Ruth hit 60 home runs in a **single** season.

5. Many fans remembered Jackie Robinson as the first **black** player in professional baseball.

6. Roger Maris is the **one** hitter who beat Babe Ruth's record.

7. Do you know the name of the **oldest** pitcher in baseball?

Remember, an adjective usually comes right before the noun it modifies.

Roger Maris

B Writing Adjectives

Use one of the adjectives in the box to complete each sentence. The adjective you choose should answer the question in parentheses.

old	other	childhood	two	round

1. The game of baseball comes from a very _____ sport called "rounders."   (**What kind of sport?**)

2. Just as in baseball, there were _____ teams in rounders. (**How many teams?**)

3. In rounders, the fielders threw the ball at the base runners on the

   _____ team.   (**Which team?**)

4. If the _____ ball hit the unlucky base runner, he or she was out.   (**What kind of ball?**)

5. In some ways, rounders is like the _____ games of tag and dodgeball.   (**What kind of games?**)

Complete the sentences you are sure of first. Mark off the adjectives as you use them. Then go back to the sentences that you left blank. See if you can find the correct adjective left on the list.

Number Missed	0	1	2	3	4	5	6	7	8	9	10	11	12
Percent Correct	100	92	83	75	67	58	50	42	33	25	17	8	0

C Adding Adjectives

Sometimes more than one adjective is used with a noun: <u>deep</u>, <u>dark</u> secret; <u>old</u> and <u>wise</u> woman. Each of the following sentences already has one adjective. Choose the best adjective in parentheses to complete each pair.

1. The pitcher threw a _____ and wild curveball. (**lazy, fast**)

2. We ate salty, _____ popcorn. (**fresh, hard**)

3. Benson is a _____, clever base-runner. (**strange, good**)

4. He is also an intelligent, _____ base-stealer.
(**sleepy, speedy**)

5. My sister has complete, _____ information about every player on the team. (**comfortable, accurate**)

D Proofreading

Correct the errors in the following paragraph. Cross out each error and write the correction above it. If punctuation needs to be added, put the marks where they should go. There are six errors. The first error is marked. You should find five more.

Hall
The Baseball ~~hall~~ of Fame is in Cooperstown, New York. It is believed that Abner Doubleday invented baseball in Cooperstown in 1839. Each year members are elected to the Baseball Hall of fame In most cases, players have to be retired for at least five years. they must also have play at least 10 year in the major leagues. The Baseball Hall of Fame began when Babe Ruth and four others were chosen as the greatest players.

E Writing Sentences

Write an answer to each of the following questions. Use at least one adjective in each of your answers.

1. How was the baseball game you saw last night? _____

_____

2. Why did the catcher drop that pitch? _____

_____

3. Why did the coach put in a different pitcher? _____

_____

Notice that two adjectives together are separated by a comma. The comma takes the place of the word <u>and</u>.

You should find and correct the following errors:
- 1 missing end punctuation mark
- 2 words that need to be capitalized
- 1 incorrect noun form
- 1 incorrect verb form

Try It Answers for page 55

1. teams
2. players
3. time

Number Missed	0	1	2	3	4	5	6	7	8	9	10	11	12	13
Percent Correct	100	92	85	77	69	62	54	46	38	31	23	15	8	0

Focus on Writing

Writing a Thank-You Note

When somebody does something nice for you, it is always a good idea to thank him or her. A **thank-you note** has the same form as a friendly letter. The only difference is that the body of a thank-you note is always very brief and to the point.

(**Heading**) 1714 272nd Street
New York, NY 10081
July 17, 1989

Dear Mr. Ramirez, (**Greeting**)
My sister Val and I want you to know how very much we enjoyed being at Yankee Stadium with you last Friday night.
It was a great thrill to see the famous players in person. Val (**Body**) and I also thought that the hot dogs, soda, and popcorn were out of this world, too.
Thank you again for such a wonderful evening.
(**Closing**) Yours truly,
(**Signature**) *Nancy Wingu*

Follow these steps to write a thank-you note.
- Write the heading. Use your own address and today's date.
- Write the letter to someone who has done something nice for you recently.
- Write a closing and sign your thank-you note.

Use one of the following closings if the person is not a relative or close friend your age: "Yours truly" or "Sincerely yours." If the person is a relative or friend your age, use a more informal closing, such as "Your nephew" or "Your pal."

Your thank-you note should have three paragraphs. In the first paragraph, thank the person and mention the event or gift. In the second, explain why you enjoyed the gift. Repeat your thanks in the third paragraph.

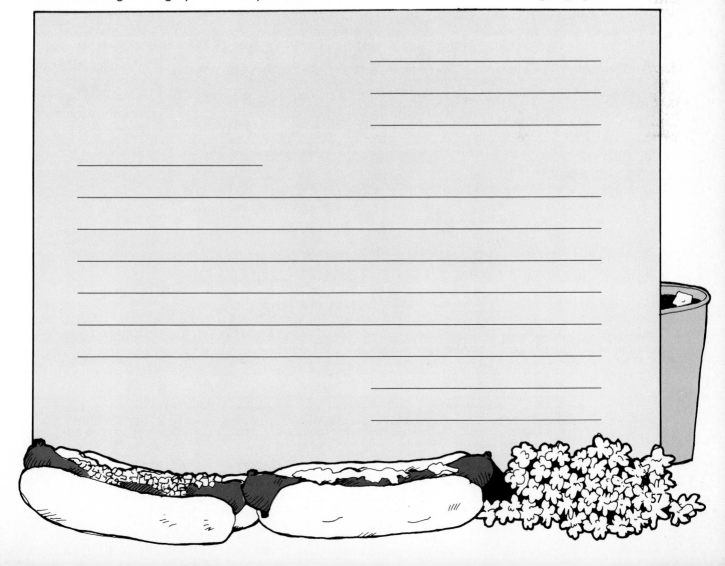

Adverbs

The Nobel Prizes

Alfred Bernhard Nobel (noh BEL) was a Swedish inventor. In 1867, he invented dynamite. Within a few years, he was one of the world's richest men. He decided to leave his money to people who had done things that helped others. Two weeks before he died, he established the Nobel Prizes. The prizes are given in fields such as medicine, literature, and economics. Nobel died on December 10, 1896. On that day, winners are given a gold medal, and a cash award. American winners do not pay taxes on that money. In 1984, the value of each prize was about $192,000.

Read the story carefully. Study the words before and after each underlined word. They will help you understand what the underlined word means.

Building Vocabulary Circle the letter of the word or words in the box below that mean almost the same as the underlined words.

1. <u>inventor</u>	a. one who watches an event	c. something that is new
	b. one who makes something new	d. person in business
2. <u>dynamite</u>	a. a food b. a toy	c. a machine d. an explosive
3. <u>established</u>	a. started b. won	c. bought d. stopped

Check your choices in a dictionary. Add these words and their meanings to your vocabulary notebook. Try to use them as often as possible.

An **adverb** is a word that modifies, or tells about, a verb, an adjective, or another adverb. An adverb may come before or after the word it modifies. It often answers the questions "When?", "Where?", and "How?"

• Nobel died **suddenly**. (modifies verb <u>died</u>; answers question "When?")

• He worked **very** hard. (modifies adverb <u>hard</u>; answers question "How?")

• He was a **truly** remarkable person. (modifies adjective <u>remarkable</u>; answers question "How much?")

Most adverbs end in **-ly**. The following words are also adverbs.

very	rather	quite	late	slow	here	well
often	never	sometimes	fast	loud	too	soon
below	down	besides	also	always	now	almost

Try It

The words in dark type are adverbs. Underline the word that each adverb modifies. Check your answers on page 60.

1. Alfred Nobel worked **hard** to invent dynamite.

2. He became a **very** rich man.

3. He felt that dynamite could **easily** harm people.

4. He wanted to make up for any harm he caused **accidentally**.

5. He died **too** soon to see anyone win one of the Nobel Prizes.

This is a warm-up exercise. If you make two or more mistakes, read the definitions and examples on page 58 again before working exercise A.

A Identifying Words That Modify Adverbs

The words in dark type are adverbs. Underline the word or words each adverb modifies.

1. The king of Sweden presents a Nobel Prize for literature **yearly**.

2. No one **ever** received the Nobel Prize for peace during World War I or World War II.

3. Someone **always** wins a prize in the field of medicine.

4. The Nobel Prize for peace was **first** presented in 1901.

5. **Sometimes** two or more people share a Nobel prize for their work in the same field.

Before you begin, review the examples on page 58.

Winner Bishop Tutu

B Identifying Adverbs

Underline the adverb in each of the following sentences. Each sentence contains one adverb.

1. A transistor is barely the size of a pencil eraser.

2. Transistors are now used to transfer electrical signals in radios.

3. TVs and other electric machines also use transistors.

4. Three Americans worked tirelessly to invent the transistor.

5. They finally finished their work in 1947.

6. Transistors quickly replaced tubes used in radios and TVs.

7. Transistors are smaller and often save on power.

8. Without transistors, radios and TVs would cost more.

9. Because transistors are small, manufacturers can also make pocket calculators.

10. The three Americans eventually won a Nobel Prize for their invention.

Hint: Look for words ending in -*ly*. Look also at those words listed in the box on page 58. In sentence 8, what word answers the question "How much?"

Number Missed	0	1	2	3	4	5	6	7	8	9	10	11	12	13	14	15	16
Percent Correct	100	94	88	81	75	69	63	56	50	44	38	31	25	19	13	6	0

C Writing
Adverbs

Write an adverb to complete each sentence. Use an adverb that ends in **-ly** or an adverb from the box on page 58. The adverb you add should answer the question in parentheses after each sentence.

More than one adverb may fit in each blank. If the word you add makes sense, you have added an adverb.

1. We _____ win when Claire pitches.   (**How often?**)

2. The train from Chicago will arrive _____.   (**When?**)

3. The members completed the meeting _____.   (**How?**)

4. I was standing _____ when the bell rang.   (**Where?**)

5. The police blocked off that _____ dangerous road.
(**How much?**)

D Proofreading

Correct the errors in the following paragraph. Cross out each error and write the correction above it. If punctuation needs to be added, put the marks where they belong. There are six errors. The first error is marked. You should find five more.

Winner Marie Curie

                    was
Sinclair Lewis ~~were~~ the first american to win a Nobel Prize in literature.

He got the award in 1930 for his novels In 1936, Eugene O'Neill won the

award for their plays. Pearl S. Buck was the third American to win an award

in literature during the 1930s. She won for her fine novels. at least four

other Americans have won awards in literature since the Nobel Prizes were

first given out. The last two win was Saul Bellow.

You should find and correct the following errors:
• 1 end mark missing
• 1 incorrect pronoun form
• 1 misspelled word
• 2 words that should be capitalized

E Writing
Sentences

Answer the following questions. Use at least one adverb in each of your answers. Underline each adverb you use. For help answering the questions, see the paragraphs on page 58 and exercise A.

1. How often are Nobel Prizes given? _____

_____

2. How often does someone win a prize in literature? _____

_____

3. When was the Nobel Prize for peace first presented? _____

_____

Try It Answers
for page 59

1. worked
2. rich
3. harm
4. caused
5. soon

Number Missed	0	1	2	3	4	5	6	7	8	9	10	11	12	13
Percent Correct	100	92	85	77	69	62	54	46	38	31	23	15	8	0

Focus on Writing

Writing an Invitation

An informal invitation follows the same form as a friendly letter. The body of the invitation must clearly tell the following: The <u>kind</u> of event it is. <u>When</u> it will take place. <u>Where</u> it will take place. Other facts that the person invited will have to know.

An informal invitation has a heading, a greeting, a body, a closing, and a signature.

(**Heading**) 18 Rolling Ridge Drive
Midland, OR 78431
August 18, 1989

Dear Gretchen, (**Greeting**)
    You are invited to an outdoor cookout at my house on Saturday, September 6. A volleyball game begins at 5:00 P.M., and lots of good food will be served at 7:00 P.M.
    Please bring your favorite record or tape. Please let me know (**Body**) by August 30 if you can't come.
                    (**Closing**) Your friend,
                    (**Signature**) Dane

Your letter will have two or three paragraphs. In the first paragraph, describe the event and include all the necessary information. If the guest should bring something special, put this information in the second paragraph. The final paragraph should tell the person when to contact you if he or she can't attend.

Follow these steps to write an invitation.
• Write the heading. Use your address and today's date.
• Choose a real or imaginary person to write to.
• In the body of your invitation, invite the person to an event of your choosing.
• Add the closing and signature.

PARTY!

Pryepositions

U.S. Army Camel Corps

In the 1850s, the U.S. Army had a <u>problem</u> getting <u>supplies</u> to its bases in the West. Someone said they should use camels.

In 1855, Congress voted $30,000 to buy camels. Two years later the Army owned 75 of those animals. In March of 1857, the first U.S. Army Camel Corps (KOR) was formed. By the end of the first year, the new corps had moved huge amounts of supplies. It opened a new road to the Pacific and traveled 4,000 miles without accident. Another 1,000 camels were ordered. Then the Civil War broke out. The idea of the Camel Corps was set aside.

Other people used the camels after that. They <u>delivered</u> mail and worked in salt mines. But their days in the Army had come to an end.

Building Vocabulary Circle the letter of the word or words in the box below that mean almost the same as the underlined words.

1. <u>problem</u>	a. base	b. way	c. person	d. difficulty
2. <u>supplies</u>	a. goods	b. men	c. forts	d. prisoners
3. <u>delivered</u>	a. stamped	b. wrote	c. took	d. asked for

A **preposition** is a word that ties a noun or pronoun to some other word. Most prepositions show <u>position</u> or <u>direction</u>. The following are very common prepositions.

about	against	at	between	for	of	to	up
above	along	before	by	from	on	toward	upon
across	among	behind	down	in	over	under	with
after	around	beside	during	into	through	until	without

A **prepositional phrase** is a group of words that begins with a preposition and ends with a noun or pronoun. The noun or pronoun is called the **object** of the preposition. When a pronoun is the object of a preposition, the object form of the pronoun is used: <u>me</u>, <u>you</u>, <u>him</u>, <u>her</u>, <u>it</u>, <u>us</u>, <u>you</u>, <u>them</u>. Other words may come between the preposition and its object.

- **behind us**   - **over** the high **mountain**   - **in** the **house**

dromedary camel

Read the story carefully. Study the words before and after each underlined word. They will help you understand what the underlined word means.

Check your choices in a dictionary. Add these words and their meanings to your vocabulary notebook. Try to use them as often as possible.

For a complete list of prepositions, see page 154 in the Handbook.

Try It

The prepositions in the following sentences are printed in dark type. Underline the object of each preposition. Check your answers on page 64.

1. Soldiers **on** camels were strange sights here.

2. No one knew if camels would work well **with** the Army.

3. The sight **of** camels frightened the settlers.

This is a warm-up exercise. If you make one or more mistakes, read the definitions and examples on page 62 again before working exercise A.

A Identifying Prepositions

Draw one line under the prepositions in the following sentences. Draw two lines under the object of each preposition. In the first three sentences, the prepositions are printed in dark type.

1. An Army study discovered the usefulness **of** camels.

2. The choice **between** horses and camels was clear **to** them.

3. Time **after** time, one camel could do the work **of** four horses.

4. A camel could carry 600 pounds a distance of 30 miles in one day.

5. The Army brought camels to this country by ship.

6. One camel that was too tall would not fit into the ship.

7. Workers cut a hole through the deck of the ship for his hump.

Notice that some sentences have more than one preposition. There are three prepositions in sentence 7.

B Writing Prepositional Phrases

Choose a prepositional phrase from the box to complete each sentence. Write the phrase in the space in each sentence.

| for their own gain | of water | about it |
| of money | in their humps | with the amount |

1. The camel story was unusual, and newspapers went wild _____.

2. Camels usually drink 20 or 30 gallons _____ at one time.

3. When they eat, fat is stored _____.

4. Their humps grow or shrink _____ they eat.

5. Some people felt the Camel Corps was a waste _____.

6. Others said the Army officers used the camels _____.

Complete the sentences you are sure of first. Mark off the phrases as you use them. Then go back to the sentences you left blank. See if you can find the correct phrase left on the list.

Number Missed	0	1	2	3	4	5	6	7	8	9	10	11	12	13	14	15	16	17	18	19	20	21	22	23	24	25	26	27	28	29	30	31	32	33
Percent Correct	100	97	94	91	88	85	82	79	76	73	70	67	64	61	58	55	52	48	45	42	39	36	33	30	27	24	21	18	15	12	9	6	3	0

Lesson 14   Part 3   Prepositions

C Writing Pronoun Objects of Prepositions — Choose the correct pronoun form in parentheses to complete each prepositional phrase. Write the correct form on the blank space in each phrase.

1. against _____ (**we, us**)
2. without _____ (**she, her**)
3. behind _____ (**he, him**)
4. with _____ (**I, me**)
5. above _____ (**we, us**)
6. beside _____ (**they, them**)
7. after _____ (**he, him**)
8. about _____ (**she, her**)
9. between you and _____ (**I, me**)
10. from _____ (**we, us**)

bactrian camel

D Proofreading — Correct the errors in the following paragraph. Cross out each error and write the correction above it. If punctuation needs to be added, put the marks where they should go. There are six errors. The first error is marked. You should find five more.

miles

The camels went 65 ~~mile~~ in 8 hours. One camel that had gone 10 days without water refused a drinks. If the Civil war had not begun, the Army Camel Corps would have been larger. some of the camels were given to the city of Los Angeles They were used to carry mail and to bring supplies from San pedro. The U.S. government sold the rest of the camels.

You should find and correct the following errors:
- 1 incorrect noun form
- 1 punctuation mark missing
- 3 words that need to be capitalized

E Writing Sentences — Answer the following questions. Use at least one preposition in each answer. For help answering the questions, see the paragraphs on page 62 and exercises A and B.

1. Were the camels used in the West? _____
_____
2. How did most people react to the idea of a Camel Corps? _____
_____
3. How did the camels come to this country? _____
_____
4. Could the camels carry much weight? _____
_____

Remember to begin each sentence with a capital letter. End each sentence with the correct punctuation mark.

Try It Answers for page 63
1. camels
2. Army
3. camels

Number Missed	0	1	2	3	4	5	6	7	8	9	10	11	12	13	14	15	16	17	18	19
Percent Correct	100	95	89	84	79	74	68	63	58	53	47	42	37	32	26	21	16	11	5	0

64

Focus on Writing

Writing an Order

People order all kinds of things through the mail. When there is no order form, you must order what you want in a **business letter**. A business letter has all of the parts of a friendly letter plus one more—the **inside address**. The inside address includes the name and address of the person or company that you are writing to.

(**Heading**) 48 Hanson Road
Rising Sun, MD 21911
January 8, 1989

(**Inside Address**)

Prairie Publishing Company
79 Industrial Drive
Liberal, KS 57320

Dear Sir or Madam: (**Greeting**)

Please send me the following books from your ad in Western   (**Body**)
Trails magazine: Southwest Caravan and Camel Mail. I enclose a
money order in the amount of $23.40 to cover the cost of both
books plus shipping and handling.

I look forward to receiving these books as soon as possible.

(**Closing**) Sincerely yours,
(**Signature**) Daisey Clemens

Notice that the greeting of a business letter ends with a colon. "Dear Sir or Madam" is a good greeting to use when you do not know the name of the person you are writing to.

The closing of a business letter is always "Sincerely yours" or "Yours truly."

Mention that you saw the company's ad. Then identify what you want. Tell what you are sending in the second paragraph.

Follow these steps to write a business letter that orders something.
- Write to: Moneysworth, 16 Francis Place, Rome, Ohio 43605.
- Order the following: I pair of roller skates, men's, black, size 9, catalog number 6F23274F. The skates cost $47. Add $2.50 for shipping.

Complete Sentences

Shortcut Between Oceans

In 1914, the United States finished the Panama Canal. The canal crosses the country of Panama. It connects the Atlantic Ocean with the Pacific Ocean. Before the canal was built, ships had to sail more than 13,000 miles to go from New York to San Francisco. After the canal opened, they had less than 5,200 miles to go.

Building the Panama Canal was not easy. Doctors had to <u>eliminate</u> diseases in the area before work could begin. As many as 43,000 workers had to be <u>recruited</u>. They removed, or <u>excavated</u>, millions of tons of rock and dirt. The canal cost about 380 million dollars. The French started digging it in 1882. The United States opened it 38 years later.

The Panama Canal is one of the great building <u>feats</u> of all time.

Read the story carefully. Study the words before and after each underlined word. They will help you understand what the underlined word means.

Building Vocabulary   Circle the letter of the word or words in the box below that mean almost the same as the underlined words.

1. <u>eliminate</u>	a. remove	b. discover	c. begin	d. create
2. <u>recruited</u>	a. counted	b. sent out	c. found	d. removed
3. <u>excavated</u>	a. filled in	b. discovered	c. rented	d. dug out
4. <u>feats</u>	a. problems	b. failures	c. hopes	d. remarkable deeds

Check your choices in a dictionary. Add these words and their meanings to your vocabulary notebook. Try to use them as often as possible.

A **sentence** is a group of words that tells a whole thought. Every sentence has a subject and a predicate. The **subject** is the person, place, or thing being talked about. The **predicate** tells what the subject is or does.

Subject

• The person I met last week

• He

Predicate

was in a show his school put on.

sang.

The whole subject is called the **complete subject**. The whole predicate is called the **complete predicate**. Note that the complete subject and the complete predicate may be one word or many words.

Try It   Draw one line under each complete subject. Draw two lines under each complete predicate. Check your answers on page 68.

1. The Panama Canal stretches for more than 50 miles.

2. The canal has three sets of chambers, called locks.

3. The length of each lock is 1,000 feet.

This is a warm-up exercise. If you make one or more mistakes, read the definitions and examples on page 66 again before working exercise A.

A Identifying Complete Subjects and Predicates

Draw one line under each complete subject. Draw two lines under each complete predicate.

1. Ships from all over the world use the Panama Canal.

2. Many American workers run the canal smoothly.

3. In 1991 the country of Panama will take control of the canal.

4. The Panama Canal is too small for many modern ships.

5. Many people want to make the canal bigger.

6. Other people want a completely new canal.

7. A canal is necessary to protect the Atlantic and Pacific coasts.

8. Without a canal the United States would need two separate navies.

9. A canal in Central America saves everyone time and money.

Remember, the subject is what the sentence is about. It may be one word or many. The predicate tells about the subject. It also may be one word or many.

B Writing Complete Subjects

Choose one of the complete subjects in the box to finish each sentence that follows.

| Swimmers through the canal | A man | The highest amount |
| The price of passage through the canal | | In 1962 that ship |

1. _____ depends on a ship's size.

2. _____ was paid by the supertanker *U.S.S. Orion Hunter.*

3. _____ paid $30,446 to go through the canal.

4. _____ had to pay only 45 cents.

5. _____ swam through the canal in December of 1962.

Complete the sentences you are sure of first. Cross out the subjects in the box as you use them. Then see if you can find the correct subjects left on the list. Be sure to capitalize the first word.

Number Missed	0	1	2	3	4	5	6	7	8	9	10	11	12	13	14	15	16	17	18	19	20	21	22	23
Percent Correct	100	96	91	87	83	78	74	70	65	61	57	52	48	43	39	35	30	26	22	17	13	9	4	0

Lesson 15   Part 3   Complete Sentences ■■■■■■■■■■■■■■■

C Writing
Complete Predicates

Choose one of the complete predicates from the box to finish each sentence. Use each predicate only once.

> **made work in Panama dangerous.**
> **could begin.**
> **asked Dr. Gorgas to make the area safe.**

1. Disease-carrying mosquitoes _____

_____

2. The United States _____

_____

3. With disease no longer a problem, work on the canal _____

_____

Complete the sentences you are sure of first. Cross out the predicates in the box as you use them. Then go back to the sentences that you left blank. See if you can find the correct predicates left on the list.

D Proofreading

Correct the errors in the following paragraph. Cross out each error and write the correction above it. If punctuation needs to be added, put the marks where they should go. There are six errors. The first error is marked. You should find five more.

                              canal
    The first ship through the ~~canel~~ was the *S.S. Ancon*. The *Ancon* sailed from the Atlantic ocean to the Pacific Ocean. Its proved the saying, "The land divided, the world united." a landslide close the canal in 1915. President woodrow Wilson reopened the canal on July 12, 1920.

Find and correct the following errors:
- **1 incorrect verb form**
- **1 incorrect pronoun form**
- **3 words that should be capitalized**

E Writing
Sentences

Answer the following questions, using complete sentences. For help in answering the questions, see the paragraphs on page 66 and exercises A and D.

1. Why do ships use the Panama Canal? _____

_____

2. What country started to dig the canal? _____

_____

3. How much did the canal cost? _____

_____

Try It Answers for page 67

1. The Panama Canal stretches for more than 50 miles.
2. The canal has three sets of chambers, called locks.
3. The length of each lock is 1,000 feet.

Number Missed	0	1	2	3	4	5	6	7	8	9	10	11
Percent Correct	100	91	82	73	64	55	45	36	27	18	9	0

Focus on Writing

Writing for Information

Another common type of business letter is one which asks for information. There are a number of reasons why you might have to request information. You might, for example, write to a travel club to ask for information about a trip you are planning.

See page 65 for information on the six parts of a business letter.

Your letter should have two paragraphs. Request what you want in the first paragraph and briefly explain why you need the information. Thank the provider of the information in advance in the second paragraph.

Follow these steps to write a letter that asks for information.
- Write the heading. Use your own address and today's date.
- Write to the following organization: Department of Tourism, State of New Mexico, State Office Building, Santa Fe, NM 87240.
- Point out that you are planning a vacation in the state. Ask for information about recreational areas. Ask for information about places to stay. Also, request a road map.

A Writing Object
Pronouns

Complete each sentence. Use an object pronoun instead of the word or words in parentheses. For help, review page 50.

1. We told (**Jack, Rita, and Sue**) _____ to be ready by eight o'clock.

2. Henry, I've given (**Henry**) _____ the last of the food.

3. Kim said, "Please give (**Kim**) _____ your address, Jeanne."

4. I asked Peter to loan (**Wallace and me**) _____ his bicycle.

5. Father called (**mother and Uncle Carlos**) _____ to breakfast.

6. Sharon, I promise to call (**Sharon**) _____ and (**Tabitha**)

   _____ this evening.

7. I think Father will let (**the person speaking**) _____ take the car,

   if I ask (**Father**) _____ nicely.

8. Mr. Salvo is going to take (**me and a group of my friends**) _____ for a tour of his company.

B Identifying
Adjectives

Underline each adjective in the following sentences. There are two adjectives in each sentence. For help, review page 54.

1. It was a dark, stormy night.

2. The sailor pulled an old map out of the wooden chest.

3. A gigantic dog guarded the tiny room.

4. In the large jar there were only three quarters.

5. A strong wind knocked over the new fence.

C Identifying
Adverbs

Underline the adverbs in the following sentences. Circle the word each adverb modifies. Two of the sentences have two adverbs. For help, review page 58.

1. Bertha quickly gained on the lead runner.

2. The wind howled loudly, but they slept soundly.

3. He sings pleasantly, but he never remembers the words.

4. The tide slowly carried the boat toward the bay.

5. I sometimes miss my friends in Texas.

Number Missed	0	1	2	3	4	5	6	7	8	9	10	11	12	13	14	15	16	17	18	19	20	21	22	23	24	25	26	27	28	29	30	31	32	33	34
Percent Correct	100	97	94	91	88	85	82	79	76	74	71	68	65	62	59	56	53	50	47	44	41	38	35	32	29	26	24	21	18	15	12	9	6	3	0

D Identifying Prepositional Phrases

Underline each prepositional phrase in the following sentences. Circle the object of the preposition. Six sentences have two prepositional phrases. For help, review page 62.

1. The dog crawled under the house.

2. The argument is between them.

3. The birds flew between the branches of the maple trees.

4. He leaned against the door and stared at the mountain.

5. Under the new rules, we cannot run up the stairs.

6. I don't know anything about him.

7. He had been walking through the woods since daylight.

8. Into every life some rain must fall.

9. Around one corner of the house was a garage.

10. We will be on vacation for a week.

11. I write to my grandmother once a week.

12. Far above the tree tops, clouds race along.

13. When it began raining, we ran for cover.

E Identifying Subjects and Predicates

Draw one line under each complete subject in the following sentences. Draw two lines under each complete predicate. For help, review page 66.

1. Last Halloween my neighbor's little boy dressed up like a tramp.

2. I saw many clowns and wild animal acts at the circus.

3. The voters in our town went to a meeting at the high school.

4. The old dog was hard of hearing and blind.

5. The last flock of Canadian geese flew north in late fall.

6. You and I must study hard for the test.

7. The team's winning streak finally ended.

8. A small, wet insect crawled out of the water onto a flat rock.

9. In the early evening hours, the fire was discovered.

10. Many singers write their own songs.

11. The most wonderful thing happened yesterday.

Number Missed	0	1	2	3	4	5	6	7	8	9	10	11	12	13	14	15	16	17	18	19	20	21	22	23	24	25	26	27	28	29	30	31	32	33	34
Percent Correct	100	98	97	95	93	92	90	88	87	85	83	82	80	78	77	75	73	72	70	68	67	65	63	62	60	58	57	55	53	52	50	48	47	45	43

Number Missed	35	36	37	38	39	40	41	42	43	44	45	46	47	48	49	50	51	52	53	54	55	56	57	58	59	60
Percent Correct	42	40	38	37	35	33	32	30	28	27	25	23	22	20	18	17	15	13	12	10	8	7	5	3	2	0

A Object Forms of Pronouns   Find the letter of the pronoun that could be used in place of the word or words in parentheses. Blacken the circle of your choice in the answer box to the right.

Answer Box

1. Let's write (**the students in that school**) a letter today.
   a. them   b. they   c. their   d. theirs   1. ⓐ ⓑ ⓒ ⓓ

2. Now I would like you to give (**the speaker**) your attention.
   a. mine   b. my   c. I   d. me   2. ⓐ ⓑ ⓒ ⓓ

3. They think that their school can beat (**our school**) in football.
   a. we   b. her   c. us   d. them   3. ⓐ ⓑ ⓒ ⓓ

4. When we see Donald, we will tell (**Donald**) to call you.
   a. he   b. his   c. him   d. them   4. ⓐ ⓑ ⓒ ⓓ

B Adjectives   Find the letter of the adjective in each sentence. Blacken the circle of your choice in the answer box to the right.

5. The sun looked like a fiery ball.
   a. sun   b. looked   c. fiery   d. ball   5. ⓐ ⓑ ⓒ ⓓ

6. The nurse carefully picked up the tiny baby from its bed.
   a. nurse   b. carefully   c. picked   d. tiny   6. ⓐ ⓑ ⓒ ⓓ

7. The heavy weight of a sack of grain weighed him down.
   a. heavy   b. weight   c. sack   d. grain   7. ⓐ ⓑ ⓒ ⓓ

8. Smoking is not allowed today in many buildings.
   a. Smoking   b. allowed   c. today   d. many   8. ⓐ ⓑ ⓒ ⓓ

C Adverbs   The words in dark type are adverbs. Find the letter of the word that each adverb modifies. Blacken the circle of your choice in the answer box to the right.

9. He **carefully** assembled the pieces of the puzzle.
   a. He   b. assembled   c. pieces   d. puzzle   9. ⓐ ⓑ ⓒ ⓓ

10. He had built a **very** fast car for the Fourth of July race.
    a. built   b. fast   c. car   d. for   10. ⓐ ⓑ ⓒ ⓓ

11. He asked the question **politely** but got no answer.
    a. asked   b. question   c. got   d. answer   11. ⓐ ⓑ ⓒ ⓓ

12. The guests arrived **late** for the party.
    a. guests   b. arrived   c. late   d. party   12. ⓐ ⓑ ⓒ ⓓ

13. She glanced **quickly** at the door and then turned away.
    a. glanced   b. door   c. turned   d. away   13. ⓐ ⓑ ⓒ ⓓ

Number Missed	0	1	2	3	4	5	6	7	8	9	10	11	12	13
Percent Correct	100	92	85	77	69	62	54	46	38	31	23	15	8	0

D Prepositional Phrases

Find the letter of the prepositional phrase that contains each preposition in dark type. Blacken the circle of your choice in the answer box to the right.

Answer Box

1. Christopher found his toy **under** the sofa in the living room.
   a. his toy under
   b. his toy under the sofa
   c. under the sofa
   d. under the sofa in the living room

   1. ⓐ ⓑ ⓒ ⓓ

2. They set up a lemonade stand **at** a bend in the road.
   a. lemonade stand at
   b. stand at
   c. at a bend
   d. at a bend in the road

   2. ⓐ ⓑ ⓒ ⓓ

3. Birds **in** the forest fly between trees without harm.
   a. Birds in the forest
   b. in the forest
   c. in the forest fly
   d. in the forest fly between

   3. ⓐ ⓑ ⓒ ⓓ

4. Anthony took the boys **for** a ride in his new car.
   a. took the boys for
   b. boys for a ride
   c. for a ride
   d. for a ride in his

   4. ⓐ ⓑ ⓒ ⓓ

5. I have not gone **beyond** the edge of the forest since July of last year.
   a. beyond
   b. beyond the edge
   c. beyond the edge of
   d. have not gone beyond

   5. ⓐ ⓑ ⓒ ⓓ

E Sentences

Find the letter for the name of each underlined word or group of words. Blacken the circle of your choice in the answer box to the right.

6. A well-known singer <u>is going to come to our town to perform</u>.
   a. complete sentence
   b. complete subject
   c. complete predicate
   d. prepositional phrase

   6. ⓐ ⓑ ⓒ ⓓ

7. <u>I</u> wonder what time the bus leaves for Redwood City.
   a. complete sentence
   b. complete subject
   c. complete predicate
   d. prepositional phrase

   7. ⓐ ⓑ ⓒ ⓓ

8. Many of my friends <u>paint</u>.
   a. complete sentence
   b. complete subject
   c. complete predicate
   d. prepositional phrase

   8. ⓐ ⓑ ⓒ ⓓ

9. The gardens <u>around the house</u> were filled with beautiful flowers.
   a. complete sentence
   b. complete subject
   c. complete predicate
   d. prepositional phrase

   9. ⓐ ⓑ ⓒ ⓓ

10. <u>Planes, trains, cars, and buses</u> move people from place to place.
    a. complete sentence
    b. complete subject
    c. complete predicate
    prepositional phrase

    10. ⓐ ⓑ ⓒ ⓓ

Number Missed	0	1	2	3	4	5	6	7	8	9	10
Percent Correct	100	90	80	70	60	50	40	30	20	10	0

Simple Subjects and Simple Predicates

An Old Friend

The automobile is not a new <u>invention</u>. A car that ran on steam first appeared in 1770. It could speed along at three miles per hour. It had to stop every 10 or 15 minutes to build up steam.

The electric car came into use during the late 1800s. It was easier to drive than the steam car. It was also faster. Sometimes it reached speeds as fast as 20 miles per hour. People could not go very far in an electric car. Its batteries had to be <u>recharged</u> about every 50 miles.

The first gasoline car appeared in 1863. It could travel six miles in two hours. The first <u>modern</u> gasoline engine was built in 1885.

In 1901, new ways were found to make cars quickly and <u>economically</u>. This meant that one day every family could own a car.

> Read the story carefully. Study the words before and after each underlined word. They will help you understand what the underlined word means.

Building Vocabulary   Circle the letter of the word or words in the box below that mean almost the same as the underlined words.

1. <u>invention</u>	a. something discovered b. something forgotten	c. explanation d. something bought
2. <u>recharged</u>	a. not paid for b. run down	c. ran again d. powered again
3. <u>modern</u>	a. automatic b. present-time	c. old-time d. powerful
4. <u>economically</u>	a. safely b. carelessly	c. constantly d. inexpensively

> Check your choices in a dictionary. Add these words and their meanings to your vocabulary notebook. Try to use them as often as you can.

The **simple subject** is the most important word or words in the complete subject. It is always a noun or pronoun. The **simple predicate** is the most important word or words in the complete predicate. It is always a verb. In the examples, a slanted line divides the complete subject from the complete predicate. The simple subjects and predicates are in dark type.

- A metal **crank / started** early cars.

- The **Pierce Arrow / was made** from 1901 to 1938.

> The simple subject names the person(s) or thing(s) the sentence is about. The simple predicate is a verb that tells what the subject is or is doing.

Try It

A line separates the complete subject from the complete predicate in each sentence below. Draw one line under each simple subject and two lines under each simple predicate. Check your answers on page 76.

1. Cars with steam engines / upset many people.

2. Those automobiles / frightened horses.

3. At the same time, steam cars / filled the air with smoke.

4. Hot coals from their fires / started blazes on wooden bridges.

This is a warm-up exercise. If you make two or more mistakes, read the definitions and examples on page 74 again before working exercise A.

A Identifying Simple Subjects and Predicates

Draw one line under each simple subject and two lines under each simple predicate in the following sentences. In the first five sentences, a line separates the complete subject from the complete predicate.

1. More than one hundred American companies / built steam automobiles.

2. The Stanley twins / made a very popular car.

3. The builders / called it the Stanley Steamer.

4. Many people / feared automobiles with steam engines.

5. They / worried about the open fire and the steam.

6. The batteries of an electric car powered it for about 50 miles.

7. Before long, drivers favored the gasoline car.

8. In 1916, a Model T automobile cost less than $400.

9. Henry Ford's company sold more than 15 million Model Ts.

10. In 1912, the first car with an electric starter appeared.

Remember, the simple subject is the noun or pronoun that names what the sentence is about. The simple predicate is the verb that tells what the simple subject does, is doing, did, or will do.

B Writing Simple Subjects

Use one of the words in the box as a simple subject in each of the following sentences.

collector	months	museums	rebuilder

1. Some _____ in the United States display old cars.

2. A serious _____ searches for beautiful old cars.

3. Several _____ are needed to restore an antique car.

4. An antique car _____ must work slowly and carefully.

Mark off the subjects as you use them. Then go back to the sentences with blanks. Find the correct subjects left on the list.

Number Missed	0	1	2	3	4	5	6	7	8	9	10	11	12	13	14	15	16	17	18	19	20	21	22	23	24
Percent Correct	100	96	92	88	83	79	75	71	67	63	58	54	50	46	42	38	33	29	25	21	17	13	8	4	0

Lesson 16 Part 3 Simple Subjects and Simple Predicates ■ ■ ■ ■ ■ ■ ■

C Writing
Simple Predicates

Use one of the words from the box below as a simple predicate in each of the following sentences.

permit	belong	search	prefer	excites

1. Some automobile lovers _____ cars from the 1950s.

2. Collectors _____ for Ford convertibles from those years.

3. The design of those cars _____ many restorers.

4. People interested in older cars often _____ to clubs.

5. These clubs _____ members to trade hard-to-get parts.

Complete the sentences you are sure of first. Mark off the simple predicates as you use them. Then go back to the sentences that you left blank. See if you can find the correct predicates left on the list.

D Proofreading

There are six errors in the paragraph below. Put missing punctuation marks where they belong. Cross out any other error and write the correction above it. The first error is corrected for you. You should find five more.

comes
The word automobile ~~come~~ from the Greek word auto -, meaning "self,"

and the french word mobile, meaning "moving." About 38 percent of all the

cars in the world are in the United States less than a third of these cars are

paid for with cash. In 1940, the horsepower of american cars ranged from 15

to 185. Today it ranges from 70 to 225 or more. The average car made in

this country weigh almost 3,100 pounds.

You should find and correct the following errors:
- **3 words that should be capitalized**
- **1 missing end punctuation mark**
- **1 incorrect simple predicate**

E Writing
Sentences

Answer each of the following questions in a complete sentence. Be sure each answer has a subject and a predicate. If you need help with the answers, see the story on page 74 and exercise A.

1. How fast did the early cars go? _____

_____

2. What kind of engine did the first car have? _____

_____

3. What damage did steam cars do? _____

_____

Try It Answers
for page 75

1. Cars upset
2. automobiles
   frightened
3. cars filled
4. coals started

Number Missed	0	1	2	3	4	5	6	7	8	9	10	11	12	13
Percent Correct	100	92	85	77	69	62	54	46	38	31	23	15	8	0

Focus on Writing

Writing a
Letter of
Application

A **letter of application** is a business letter that you would write to apply for a job. Read the following ad that appeared in the Help Wanted section of a newspaper.

Lawn Maintenance

Owner of four rental properties needs young man or woman to maintain lawns and grounds from May 1 to November 1. Flexible schedule. About 30 hours per week required. Must be reliable and careful worker. Good hourly rate. Equipment provided. Reply to Ms. Lois Arnez, Tower Corporation, 811 Wilson Street, Manchester, NH 09421.

Write a letter of application in response to the ad. Tell where you saw the ad in the first paragraph. Introduce yourself in the second paragraph and tell why you are writing. Mention the names of at least two people who can tell about your work habits. Say that you are available for an interview in the closing paragraph and give a phone number at which you can be reached. Use capitalization and punctuation correctly in the various parts of the business letter.

_____

_____

_____

_____

_____

_____

_____

_____

_____

_____

_____

_____

Subject-Verb Agreement

The Great Walker

Edward Payson Weston was famous for walking. It all began when he walked from Boston to Washington, D.C., to collect a <u>wager</u> he had made on President Lincoln's election. Weston covered the 478 miles in 10 days. His reward was a bag of peanuts.

After that, Weston walked for money. He won a prize of $10,000 for walking from Portland, Maine, to Chicago. He often walked 1,000 miles or more. He set such a fast pace, the <u>referees</u> who measured the distance he covered needed fresh horses to keep up with him.

In 1909, Weston <u>celebrated</u> his 70th birthday by walking from New York to San Francisco. The trip of 3,895 miles took 104 days and 7 hours. His last long-distance walk covered 1,546 miles. He was then 74 years old.

Read the story carefully. Study the words before and after each underlined word. They will help you understand what the underlined word means.

Building Vocabulary   Circle the letter of the word or words in the box below that mean almost the same as the underlined words.

1. <u>wager</u>	a. promise	b. bet	c. family member	d. friend
2. <u>referees</u>	a. competitors b. highway workers		c. sports judges d. wagon drivers	
3. <u>celebrated</u>	a. wished for	b. honored	c. gave up	d. sent for

Check your choices in a dictionary. Add these words and their meanings to your vocabulary notebook. Try to use them as often as you can.

Subjects and verbs must match, or **agree**, in sentences. Study the rules below. In the examples, the subject is in dark type. The verb is underlined.

- Singular subjects take singular verbs. The **man** <u>walks</u> for relaxation.

- Plural subjects take plural verbs. Some **men** <u>walk</u> for enjoyment.

- When the subject is either a singular noun or the pronouns <u>he</u>, <u>she</u>, or <u>it</u>, present tense verbs usually end in -**s**. My **aunt** <u>jogs</u> every day.   **She** <u>jogs</u> for at least an hour.

- The verb does not end in -s when the subject is either a plural noun or the pronouns <u>I</u>, <u>you</u>, <u>we</u>, or <u>they</u>. The **members** of the track team <u>run</u> daily.   **I** <u>run</u> as often as I can.

Hint: To help remember subject-verb agreement the rule is: "If the subject ends in -s, the verb does not. If the verb ends in -s, the subject should not." This rule only works when the subject is a regular noun.

Try It

The subject and verb below are in dark type. Draw one line under each singular subject and verb. Draw two lines under each plural subject and verb. Check your answers on page 80.

1. **Weston thinks** 20 miles is a short walk.

2. **People** in carriages **follow** the famous walker from town to town.

3. **Reporters** in every town **ask** him questions.

4. The young **man takes** only short naps on his long walks.

This is a warm-up exercise. If you make two or more mistakes, read the definitions and examples on page 78 again before working exercise A.

A Identifying Subject-Verb Agreement

Draw one line under each singular subject and verb in the following sentences. Draw two lines under each plural subject and verb. In the first five sentences, the subject and verb are in dark type.

1. The long-distance **walker leaves** Massachusetts late because of snow.

2. **People** in New York City **welcome** him on February 27, 1864.

3. **He begins** the trip to Washington a few days later.

4. Some **farmers** along the way **let** him sleep in their houses.

5. On sunny days, **Weston sleeps** beside the road.

6. Children often follow him along the road.

7. Weston sometimes snacks during his walk.

8. The tired but happy man reaches Washington in record time.

9. Crowds at President Lincoln's ball cheer Weston.

Remember, the verb agrees only with the simple subject. Disregard any words that might come between the subject and the verb.

B Writing Subjects That Agree

Choose the correct subject in parentheses to complete each sentence. Then write it in the space.

1. In 1879, the _____ beats the English walking champion in London.   (**American, Americans**)

2. The _____ cover 550 miles.   (**walker, walkers**)

3. The _____ takes six days.   (**walk, walks**)

4. Long _____ are easy for Weston.   (**walk, walks**)

5. _____ ride beside him.   (**A referee, Referees**)

6. _____ keep track of Weston's time.   (**He, They**)

First, find the verb in each sentence. Then choose the singular or plural subject that agrees with it.

Number Missed	0	1	2	3	4	5	6	7	8	9	10	11	12	13	14	15	16	17	18	19	20	21	22	23	24
Percent Correct	100	96	92	88	83	79	75	71	67	63	58	54	50	46	42	38	33	29	25	21	17	13	8	4	0

Lesson 17   Part 3   Subject-Verb Agreement ■■■■■■■■■■■■■

C Writing Verbs That Agree
Choose the correct word in parentheses to complete each sentence. Write the correct verb in the space.

First, find the subject in each sentence. Then choose the singular or plural verb that agrees with it.

1. Weston, on one of his many walks, _____ to cover more than 1,200 miles in 26 days.   (**tries**, **try**)

2. He _____ so fast that he has time to attend church services along the way.   (**walks**, **walk**)

3. Even the referees' horses _____ to keep up with him.   (**fails**, **fail**)

4. Years _____ by while Weston walks.   (**slips**, **slip**)

5. The great walker, after a long career, _____ at the age of 90. (**dies**, **die**)

D Proofreading
Correct the errors in the following paragraph. Put the missing punctuation mark where it belongs. Cross out each other error. Write the correction above it. The first one is done for you. You should find five more. Do not change present tense verbs to the past tense.

Weston's walk from New York to Minneapolis ~~are~~ *is* his last long walk. in 1927, while walking in a street, he is hit by a car. Weston is badly hurt. He spend his last two year in a wheelchair He die in 1929 at the age of 90, after a long and unusual life. For 52 years, Weston has walked here and in other countries. Hundreds of people have cheered him on.

You should find and correct the following errors:
- 1 missing punctuation mark
- 1 incorrect noun form
- 1 word that should be capitalized
- 2 subject-verb agreement errors

E Writing Sentences
Answer each of the following questions with a complete sentence. Be sure that the subject and verb agree in each sentence. If you need help with the answers, review the story on page 78 and exercises A to D. Use a present tense verb in each answer.

1. Why does Weston become famous? _____

_____

2. How do farmers help Weston? _____

_____

3. What does Weston do in London? _____

_____

Try It Answers for page 79

1. Weston thinks
2. People follow
3. Reporters ask
4. man takes

Number Missed	0	1	2	3	4	5	6	7	8	9	10	11	12	13
Percent Correct	100	92	85	77	69	62	54	46	38	31	23	15	8	0

Focus on Writing

Giving Directions

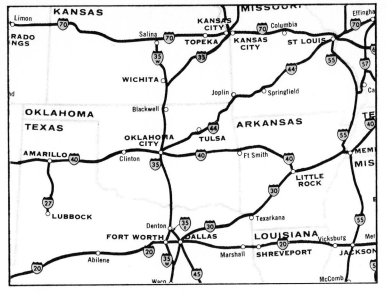

Remember to use capital letters and commas correctly in the heading, the greeting, and the closing of your letter. If you need help, review page 53.

Remember to use words and phrases to help your friend follow the directions. Use words like <u>then</u> and <u>next</u>. Use phrases like <u>to the North</u> and <u>after crossing the Mississippi River</u>.

Imagine that you live in Dallas and you have a friend who lives in St. Louis. Your friend is going to drive to Dallas to visit you. You write a friendly letter to your friend. In your letter you tell him or her what roads to take from St. Louis to Dallas. Do the following.

- In the letter's first paragraph, tell your friend that you look forward to the visit. Mention the date of the visit.
- Study the map on this page. In the letter's second paragraph, describe exactly what roads your friend should take. Be as definite as possible. Mention road names, highway numbers, exit places and numbers, and directions.
- In the final paragraph, give your phone number so that your friend can call to get local directions when he or she arrives in Dallas.

Compound Subjects and Predicates

The Last Dodo

In 1507, explorers found a strange bird on an island in the Indian Ocean. Its body was round. It had short yellow legs and a big hooked bill. It weighed about 50 pounds. It had tiny wings and could not fly. It did not seem to be very intelligent. Those who found the bird named it the dodo. They took the bird to Europe, where people flocked to see it.

When the island was settled in 1644, the dodo was doomed. Hogs, dogs, cats, and people could easily catch and eat the dodo or its eggs. By 1681, the strange bird was extinct and gone forever.

Read the story carefully. Study the words before and after each underlined word. They will help you understand what the underlined word means.

Building Vocabulary   Circle the letter of the word or words in the box below that mean almost the same as the underlined words.

1. explorers	a. farmers	b. settlers	c. searchers	d. miners
2. intelligent	a. fast flying	b. likeable	c. heavy	d. smart
3. doomed	a. discovered	b. due to die	c. caught	d. admired
4. extinct	a. no longer existing	b. accepted	c. locked up	d. alive

Check your choices in a dictionary. Add these words and their meanings to your vocabulary notebook. Try to use them as often as you can.

A sentence may have a **compound subject**. A compound subject is made up of two or more nouns or pronouns joined by the word and or or.

- When **and** joins the parts of a compound subject, the verb is plural.
  The dodo **and** the dinosaur are extinct.   The class **and** I ran.

- When or joins singular nouns or pronouns, the verb is singular.
  The captain **or** a sailor steers the ship. (one or the other, not both)

- When or joins a singular and a plural noun or pronoun, the verb agrees with the word that comes after or.
  A bus **or** two vans are enough.   Two vans **or a bus** is enough.

A sentence may also have a **compound predicate**. A compound predicate is made up of two or more verbs joined by and or or.

- The dodo looked **and** acted odd.   • Dodos hopped **or** waddled.

The words and and or are called conjunctions because they connect other words.

Try It   In each sentence below, draw one line under the compound subject and two lines under the compound predicate. Check your answers on page 84.

1. Early explorers often caught and took new animals back to their homelands.

2. A variety of strange animals and plants were carried back to the explorers' lands.

3. Sailors cooked and ate some of the dodos.

4. The captain and crew agreed they were too tough.

This is a warm-up exercise. If you make two or more mistakes, read the definitions and examples on page 82 again before working exercise A.

A Identifying Compound Subjects and Predicates   Draw one line under each compound subject in the following sentences. Draw two lines under each compound predicate.

1. One museum stuffs and displays a dodo for public viewing.

2. After a while, its head and body begin to fall apart.

3. Its feathers loosen or break.

4. The museum director or a staff member removes the bird.

5. A museum worker discards or burns most of the bird.

6. Only the head and one leg of the last dodo on Earth remain.

To find compound subjects and predicates, look for the conjunctions <u>and</u> and <u>or</u>.

B Writing Compound Subjects   Choose the compound subject in parentheses that correctly completes each sentence. Then write it in the blank.

1. _____ are not as heavy as dodos.   (**A goose or a turkey, Geese and turkeys**)

2. _____ are strange looking. (**The dodo's wings and body, The dodo's wings or body**)

3. Its _____ amuse the explorers.   (**bill and face, bill or face**)

4. _____ first captures the dodo.   (**A sailor and his dog, A sailor or his dog**)

5. Even _____ easily catch the slow-moving bird.   (**a cat or a hog, cats or hogs**)

6. _____ becomes a source of food.   (**The dodo or its eggs, The eggs or the dodo**)

Make sure each compound subject agrees with its verb. For help, review the rules and examples on page 82.

Number Missed	0	1	2	3	4	5	6	7	8	9	10	11	12
Percent Correct	100	92	83	75	67	58	50	42	33	25	17	8	0

C Writing
Compound
Predicates

Choose the compound predicate in parentheses that correctly completes each sentence. Then write it in the blank space.

1. In 1865, some scientists _____ parts of dodos in a swamp.   (**finds and collects**, **find and collect**)

2. Workers carefully _____ the bones together. (**fits and wires**, **fit and wire**)

3. Then an expert _____ a body over the bones.   (**shapes or builds**, **shape or build**)

4. An expert or trained assistants _____ feathers to the body.   (**adds and glues**, **add and glue**)

5. Today, experts and other visitors _____ the dodo in a museum.   (**comes and examines**, **come and examine**)

6. Museum guides or a book _____ the dodo's history.   (**describes and explains**, **describe and explain**)

Make sure each compound predicate agrees with its subject. For help, review page 82.

D Proofreading

Correct the errors in the following paragraph. Put punctuation marks where they belong. Cross out each error and write the correction above it. The first error is corrected. You should find five more.

It is lucky for us that the bones of dodos were found in a muddy
swamp
~~swamps~~ on the island of Mauritius. People was able to put the bones to-

gether. in that way, they were able to make more than one dodo. We can

see a dodo now when we goes to a museum It will not be a real bird, but it

will look like the real thing. The story of the dodo teach us a lesson. We

should learn not to destroy too many of one kind of animal.

You should find and correct the following errors:
- 1 word that should be capitalized
- 1 missing end punctuation mark
- 3 incorrect verb forms

E Writing
Sentences

Write two sentences of your own. Use the compound subject and the compound predicate in parentheses.

1. (**book or magazine**) _____

   _____

2. (**flap and waddle**) _____

   _____

Try It Answers for page 83

1. caught and took
2. animals and plants
3. cooked and ate
4. captain and crew

Number Missed	0	1	2	3	4	5	6	7	8	9	10	11	12	13
Percent Correct	100	92	85	77	69	62	54	46	38	31	23	15	8	0

Focus on Writing

Writing a
Brief, Brief
Report

The last dodo disappeared forever over 300 years ago. But birds also become extinct today. One such bird is the California condor. As far as anyone can tell, only a single pair remains alive today.

Imagine that you are the editor of a newspaper. As you put together one of the paper's pages, you notice that you have about three inches of blank space in one column. You decide to write a very brief report about the California condor. Use the information in the box below to write the very brief report. The information is in the form of notes. Use the information in complete sentences. The headline and the first sentence of the report are done for you.

Facts About the California Condor

largest bird in the United States … almost 5 feet long … wing-spread of from 9 to 10 feet … eats dead animals but will attack living animals as large as a deer … in trouble because female lays only one egg … will not mate until at least six years old … builds nest of twigs on the sides of steep cliffs … only one pair survives

---

Condor Update

The California condor is almost extinct. _____

_____

_____

_____

_____

_____

_____

_____

_____

_____

Talk about the bird's size and strength in the first two sentences. Then write this sentence: <u>In spite of its size and strength, the condor is about to vanish.</u> In the last two sentences, talk about what it does that endangers it.

Sentence Fragments

The First Ice Cream Cone

The Louisiana Purchase Exposition was the name of the great fair held in St. Louis, Missouri, in 1904. The first ice cream cone was made during that fair. However, we are not sure who made it. There are two stories about the ice cream cone's <u>initial</u> appearance.

One story <u>relates</u> the role that Charles E. Menches played in the invention. He was an ice cream <u>vendor</u> at the fair. One night he brought flowers and an ice cream sandwich to a lady friend. The woman had no vase, so she took one <u>layer</u> of the sandwich and rolled it into a cone shape to hold the flowers. She then rolled another cone for the ice cream.

Read the story carefully. Study the words before and after each underlined word. They will help you understand what the underlined word means.

Building Vocabulary   Circle the letter of the word or words in the box below that mean almost the same as the underlined words.

1. <u>initial</u>	a. brief	b. slow	c. first	d. late
2. <u>relates</u>	a. tells	b. ignores	c. omits	d. denies
3. <u>vendor</u>	a. buyer	b. one who cooks	c. taster	d. one who sells
4. <u>layer</u>	a. half	b. one thickness	c. bowl	d. one scoop

Check your choices in a dictionary. Add these words and their meanings to your vocabulary notebook. Try to use them as often as you can.

A **sentence fragment** is a group of words that does not express a complete thought. A sentence fragment is usually missing a subject, a predicate, or both. You can turn sentence fragments into complete sentences by supplying the missing part.

Sentence Fragments	Complete Sentences
Invented the ice cream cone in 1904. (no subject)	Someone invented the ice cream cone in 1904.
The ice cream cone immediately. (no predicate)	The ice cream cone immediately became popular.
At the end of the fair. (no subject or predicate)	The vendors relaxed at the end of the fair.

Try It

Study the groups of words below. Four groups of words are sentence fragments and one group of words is a complete sentence. After each word group, write SF for "Sentence Fragment" or S for "Sentence." Check your answers on page 88.

1. At the 1904 fair in St. Louis. _____

2. Attracted millions of people. _____

3. Are not sure of the inventor. _____

4. Charles Menches sold ice cream at the fair. _____

5. At least one other story about the first ice cream cone. _____

This is a warm-up exercise. If you make two or more mistakes, read the definitions and examples on page 86 again before working exercise A.

A Identifying Sentence Fragments

Study the groups of words below. If a group of words is a complete sentence, write S in the space that follows it. If a group of words is a sentence fragment, write SF.

1. Abe Doumar also claimed the invention of the ice cream cone. _____

2. Had an ice cream stand at the fair. _____

3. Doumar was selling a lot of ice cream to visitors. _____

4. Heard that a salesperson had run out of ice cream dishes. _____

5. Rolled up a waffle and filled it with ice cream. _____

6. Salesperson happy about idea. _____

7. Sold waffle with ice cream for ten cents. _____

8. Visitors bought the waffles with ice cream. _____

9. At the delicious treat. _____

10. Two years later, Doumar a stand at Coney Island in New York. _____

11. The ice cream cone a waffle iron for his cones. _____

12. Many people ice cream cones at Doumar's stand. _____

13. One year later, Doumar moved to Norfolk, Virginia. _____

14. Called his store there Doumar's Ice Cream Parlor. _____

15. Until his death in 1947. _____

Remember, a complete sentence must have both a simple subject and a simple predicate.

Number Missed	0	1	2	3	4	5	6	7	8	9	10	11	12	13	14	15
Percent Correct	100	93	87	80	73	67	60	53	47	40	33	27	20	13	7	0

Lesson 19 Part 3 Sentence Fragments ■■■■■■■■■■■■■

B Turning Fragments into Sentences

Write one or more of your own words to make a sentence out of each of the following fragments.

1. The first ice cream cone _____.

2. _____ was an ice cream vendor at the fair.

3. _____ loved ice cream cones from the beginning.

4. Abe Doumar _____.

5. _____ are popular with people of all ages.

Be sure that the completed sentence has <u>both</u> a simple subject <u>and</u> a simple predicate.

C Proofreading

Find the errors in the following paragraph. Put punctuation marks and missing words where they belong. Cross out any other error and write the correction above it. The first error is corrected for you. You should find five more.

　　　　　　　　　　　　　　cones
Those of us who like ice cream ~~cone~~ should be thankful for the Louisiana purchase Exposition. We knows that the ice cream cone was invented at that fair in St. Louis, missouri. The year 1904. Some salesperson at that fair invented or helped invent the ice cream cone. Do you think it was Charles E. Menches or Abe Doumar We may never know the answer.

You should find and correct the following errors:

• 2 words that should be capitalized
• 1 incorrect verb form
• 1 sentence fragment (missing verb)
• 1 missing end punctuation mark

D Writing Sentences

Answer the following questions in complete sentences. Underline the simple subject and simple predicate in each sentence you write. If you need help with the answers, read the story on page 86 and look at exercises A through C.

1. When was the first ice cream cone invented? _____

_____

2. Where was the first ice cream cone invented? _____

_____

3. What did people think about the ice cream cone? _____

_____

4. Where was Abe Doumar's second ice cream stand? _____

_____

Try It Answers for page 87

1. SF
2. SF
3. SF
4. S
5. SF

Number Missed	0	1	2	3	4	5	6	7	8	9	10	11	12	13	14
Percent Correct	100	93	86	79	71	64	57	50	43	36	29	21	14	7	0

Focus on Writing

Writing a
Letter of
Congratulations

When someone does something worthwhile, it is a nice idea to send that person a **letter of congratulations**. Thoughtful people send such letters when someone receives an honor, graduates from school, or gets a job promotion. If you know the person well, you would write a friendly letter. If the person was unknown to you, you would write a business letter.

Remember to use capitalization and punctuation correctly in the various parts of the friendly letter. If you need help, review page 53.

Imagine that you are living in the year 1904. You have just read in the newspaper that Charles E. Menches, an old friend of yours, has invented the ice-cream cone. You want to write a letter of congratulations. Do the following.
- Use your own address in the heading and the date of October 18, 1904.
- In the first paragraph, tell how you found out about the invention.
- In the second paragraph, congratulate Charles. Briefly explain why you think that what he invented is useful and worthwhile.
- Wish him well with his invention in the final paragraph of the letter.

Compound Sentences

Rock Music

Rock music is a form of <u>popular</u> music. It is now enjoyed in many parts of the world, but it began in the United States during the late 1940s. From the beginning, rock music has had a strong beat. Since both <u>performers</u> and listeners often swayed to this beat with a rocking and rolling motion, the music became known as "rock 'n roll." Most rock groups use electric guitars. One person is usually the lead singer, but the other members of the group may also sing.

From the first, rock music was popular with young people, who listened to it <u>frequently</u>. It was also young people who <u>composed</u> the music and played it. Some of these performers were well paid for their music and became wealthy while they were young. Bill Haley and His Comets were the first rock band to become famous. Their recording of "Rock Around the Clock" paved the way for such famous "rock 'n rollers" as Chuck Berry, Buddy Holly, and Little Richard.

Read the story carefully. Study the words before and after each underlined word. They will help you understand what the underlined word means.

Building Vocabulary Circle the letter of the word or words in the box below that mean almost the same as the underlined words.

1. <u>popular</u>	a. liked by many	b. hated	c. strange	d. loud
2. <u>performers</u>	a. miners	b. players	c. builders	d. fans
3. <u>frequently</u>	a. unwillingly	b. often	c. sometimes	d. quietly
4. <u>composed</u>	a. wrote	b. sang	c. listened	d. found

Check your choices in a dictionary. Add these words and their meanings to your vocabulary notebook. Try to use them as often as you can.

A **compound sentence** is made up of two or more sentences, each of which is a complete thought. They are joined together by the conjunctions <u>and</u>, <u>but</u>, or <u>or</u> to form a compound sentence. In a compound sentence, a comma always comes before the conjunction.

Remember, conjunctions are connecting words.

• Young people listen to rock music, **and** they perform rock music.

• Rock is popular today, **but** it is not a new form of music.

• People can sing rock songs, **or** they can dance to rock music.

Try It   Study the sentences below. Write CS for "Compound Sentence" after each compound sentence and circle the conjunction. Write S for "Sentence" after each word group that is not a compound sentence. Two of the sentences are compound sentences. Check your answers on page 92.

1. Rock music is very popular, but not everyone likes it. _____

2. Some groups use clouds of smoke, or they put on a light show. _____

3. Colored lights and movies are used in light shows. _____

This is a warm-up exercise. If you make one or more mistakes, read the definitions and examples on page 90 again before working exercise A.

A Identifying Compound Sentences

Find the four compound sentences below. Circle the conjunction in each one. Then draw a line through each sentence that is not a compound sentence.

1. Elvis Presley started as a country and western singer, but he became famous as a rock singer.

2. In 1956, he recorded the hit songs "Heartbreak Hotel" and "Hound Dog."

3. Bill Haley and His Comets was the first famous rock band.

4. They recorded "Rock Around the Clock", and the song became a hit.

5. Chuck Berry was a blues singer, but he wrote rock songs as well.

6. Rock music was played a great deal on radio during the mid-1950s.

7. Many people were upset by rock, or they thought it was just noise.

Bill Haley
and His Comets

B Completing Compound Sentences

Make compound sentences by combining each pair of ideas with a comma and the conjunction <u>and</u>, <u>but</u>, or <u>or</u>.

1. People expected rock groups to perform in theaters _____ the groups often played at outdoor festivals.

2. Several rock festivals were held in this country _____ they were held in other countries as well.

3. Rock music was combined with plays _____ many stage shows using rock music were produced in the late 60s.

4. Many rock songs were mainly entertaining _____ some gave listeners a very serious message.

5. In the beginning, listeners either complained about rock music _____ they thought it was the best music ever.

The word <u>and</u> in compound sentences often means <u>also</u>. The word <u>but</u> often signals a difference between ideas in the word groups that it joins. The word <u>or</u> signals that either one idea or the other is true or will happen.

Number Missed	0	1	2	3	4	5	6	7	8	9	10	11	12
Percent Correct	100	92	83	75	67	58	50	42	33	25	17	8	0

Lesson 20 Part 3 Compound Sentences ■■■■■■■■■■■■■

C Writing
Compound
Sentences

Combine each pair of sentences to form a compound sentence. Use a comma and the conjunction <u>and</u>, <u>but</u>, or <u>or</u> to join the two ideas.

1. Rock was built on the blues. It led to "heavy metal" rock. _____

   _____

2. Disco appeared in the 1970s. This new rock became very popular. _____

   _____

3. Disco was sometimes played by a live band. It was played on records at

   disco clubs. _____

   _____

4. The punk rock of the late 1970s did not last long. It led to new kinds of

   rock in the 1980s. _____

   _____

Chuck Berry

D Proofreading

Find the errors in the paragraph below. Cross out each error and write the correction above it. There are six errors. The first is corrected for you. You should find five more.

       writers
  Punk rock led ~~righters~~ to try new kinds of rock. the new kinds are usu-

ally grouped under the name New Wave. groups such as Devo and blondie

are New Wave groups. Many rock singers have put their music into short

films, or some of these films is shown on TV.

E Writing
Sentences

Answer each question with a compound sentence. For help, look at the story on page 90 and at exercises A to C.

1. What did Elvis Presley do? _____

   _____

2. Where did people hear or see rock? _____

   _____

3. What was Bill Haley famous for? _____

   _____

You should find and correct the following errors:
- **3 words that should be capitalized**
- **1 incorrect verb form**
- **1 incorrect conjunction**

Try It Answers
for page 91

1. CS
2. CS
3. S

Number Missed	0	1	2	3	4	5	6	7	8	9	10	11	12
Percent Correct	100	92	83	75	67	58	50	42	33	25	17	8	0

Focus on Writing

Writing a Fan Letter

People who perform love to receive letters from their fans. These letters let performers know that the people who watch and listen to them appreciate them. Fan letters mean that people are interested in the star. Here is a letter that an admirer wrote to the singing star Anita Melody.

18 Deerfield Court
Anchorage, AK 99517
March 13, 1989

Dear Anita,

I just wanted you to know that I think you're terrific. I heard your new album for the first time last night. Wow! It's the best I ever heard.

I am starting a fan club for you in this area. It would help a lot if you could send four or five autographed photos. Those will help me get the club off to a good start.

Your fan forever,

Debra Coles

On the lines below, write a fan letter to your favorite singer, musician, or musical group. In the body of your letter, tell the star how you feel about his or her music and why you feel as you do. Mention the song or album that you like best. Tell a few things about yourself and ask for an autographed photo of the star. Since fan letters are informal, use the friendly letter form.

Remember to use capital letters and punctuation marks correctly in the various parts of the friendly letter. If you need help, review page 53.

A Identifying Simple Subjects and Predicates

In each sentence, draw one line under the simple subject. Draw two lines under the simple predicate. For help, review page 74.

1. People from many countries came to the United States.

2. Cats are interesting pets.

3. The small boy in the large straw hat enjoys the pool.

4. Last week I went to a party.

5. Sunday is my favorite day of the week.

6. The pitcher on their team throws very well.

7. Tomorrow night I will go to the show with Grace.

8. The Conroy twins painted their bedroom walls.

9. Each day my sister runs at least five miles.

10. My uncle will arrive at our house this week.

11. A friend of my father's drives more than 20 miles to work.

12. A well-known rock star will speak at the high school.

13. Our neighbor will keep the mail for us.

14. My cousin knows everyone at the post office.

B Writing Subjects and Predicates

Circle the word in parentheses that correctly completes each sentence. Be sure that each subject agrees with the verb. For help, review page 78.

1. Most (horse, horses) eat oats and hay.

2. In my neighborhood, the older kids (play, plays) softball every afternoon.

3. Clowns in funny clothes (make, makes) us laugh at the circus.

4. As a rule, pine (tree, trees) grow slowly.

5. That dog (chase, chases) cars.

6. After a day on the beach, (I, we) are very tired.

7. It (is, are) too late to call anyone.

8. First teeth (fall, falls) out when children are very young.

9. The sun (shine, shines) brightly in the summer.

10. By April, (family, families) are planning their summer vacations.

Number Missed	0	1	2	3	4	5	6	7	8	9	10	11	12	13	14	15	16	17	18	19	20	21	22	23	24
Percent Correct	100	97	95	92	89	86	84	82	79	76	74	71	68	66	63	61	58	55	53	50	47	45	42	39	37

Number Missed	25	26	27	28	29	30	31	32	33	34	35	36	37	38
Percent Correct	34	32	29	26	24	21	18	16	13	11	8	5	3	0

C Identifying Compound Subjects and Predicates

Draw one line under each compound subject. Draw two lines under each compound predicate. For help, review page 82.

1. Harry and Sue read the same book.

2. At camp we will walk, swim, and eat great food.

3. Indians and a few scouts from the settlement have visited that island.

4. In March, my brothers, sisters, and I fly kites at the beach.

5. We study and take tests on that subject in school.

6. You must address, stamp, and mail the envelope.

7. Matthew J. Barron and I work for the same company.

8. All men, women, and children have some fears.

D Identifying Sentence Fragments

Write S for "Sentence" or SF for "Sentence Fragment" beside each group of words. For help, review page 86.

1. _____ After our company leaves at the end of the week.

2. _____ They dance.

3. _____ He and I are friends.

4. _____ Often helped his cousin Jill with the cooking.

5. _____ The big dog up the street with the loud bark.

6. _____ Dived off the big rock into the pool.

7. _____ Debbie gave Marsha a birthday gift.

8. _____ In the trunk of the new car.

E Identifying Compound Sentences

Draw a line under each compound sentence. For help, review page 90.

1. Joe, Manny, and Hank passed the time by talking and playing a game.

2. It was getting late, and Dad was worried about Wendy.

3. Tomorrow we can have a picnic, or we can eat at home.

4. Uncle Jed picked three ripe tomatoes and brought them into the house.

5. Delia and Ruth are cousins, but they do not live in the same town.

Number Missed	0	1	2	3	4	5	6	7	8	9	10	11	12	13	14	15	16	17	18	19	20	21
Percent Correct	100	95	90	86	81	76	71	67	62	57	52	48	43	38	33	29	24	19	14	10	5	0

A Simple Subjects

Find the letter of the simple subject in each sentence. Blacken the circle for that choice in the answer box to the right.

Answer Box

1. Three small kittens were playing with the ball of yarn.

    a. Three   b. small   c. kittens   d. were playing

1. ⓐ ⓑ ⓒ ⓓ

2. After lunch he built a birdhouse for the maple tree.

    a. After   b. lunch   c. he   d. built

2. ⓐ ⓑ ⓒ ⓓ

3. I run three miles each day to keep in shape.

    a. I   b. run   c. miles   d. shape

3. ⓐ ⓑ ⓒ ⓓ

B Simple Predicates

Find the letter of the simple predicate in each sentence. Blacken the circle for that choice in the answer box to the right.

4. During their vacation, the Whatleys will go to New York City.

    a. vacation   b. will   c. go   d. will go

4. ⓐ ⓑ ⓒ ⓓ

5. The boss spoke to Martin about being late.

    a. boss   b. spoke   c. Martin   d. being

5. ⓐ ⓑ ⓒ ⓓ

6. Each year the garden club plants flowers in the town square.

    a. year   b. garden   c. plants   d. square

6. ⓐ ⓑ ⓒ ⓓ

7. The hungry wolf searched the field for food.

    a. wolf   b. searched   c. field   d. for food

7. ⓐ ⓑ ⓒ ⓓ

C Subject-Verb Agreement

Find the letter of the choice that tells what change, if any, is needed to correct the subject-verb agreement in each sentence. Blacken the circle for that choice in the answer box to the right.

8. Most boys and girls of school age enjoys vacation.

    a. no change   b. change <u>boys and girls</u> to <u>boy and girl</u>
    c. change <u>most</u> to <u>each</u>   d. change <u>enjoys</u> to <u>enjoy</u>

8. ⓐ ⓑ ⓒ ⓓ

9. A tree live many years if they are not damaged.

    a. change <u>A tree</u> to <u>Trees</u>   b. change <u>they</u> to <u>it</u>
    c. change <u>are</u> to <u>is</u>   d. no change

9. ⓐ ⓑ ⓒ ⓓ

10. The house across from ours badly need paint.

    a. change <u>ours</u> to <u>our</u>   b. change <u>paint</u> to <u>paints</u>
    c. no change   d. change <u>need</u> to <u>needs</u>

10. ⓐ ⓑ ⓒ ⓓ

11. Each morning I eats a big breakfast of eggs and toast.

    a. change <u>I</u> to <u>we</u>   b. no change
    c. change <u>eats</u> to <u>eat</u>   d. change <u>morning</u> to <u>mornings</u>

11. ⓐ ⓑ ⓒ ⓓ

Number Missed	0	1	2	3	4	5	6	7	8	9	10	11
Percent Correct	100	91	82	73	64	55	45	36	27	18	9	0

D Compound
Subjects

Find the letter of the compound subject in each sentence. Blacken the circle for that choice in the answer box to the right.

1. Yesterday he and I had lunch together.

   a. Yesterday he   b. he and I   c. I had   d. had lunch

   1. ⓐ ⓑ ⓒ ⓓ

2. As a rule, dogs and cats do not get along well together.

   a. As a rule   b. dogs and cats   c. cats do   d. get along

   2. ⓐ ⓑ ⓒ ⓓ

3. Red, white, and blue are the colors of our flag.

   a. Red, white, and blue   b. white, and blue   c. and blue   d. are the colors

   3. ⓐ ⓑ ⓒ ⓓ

E Compound
Predicates

Find the letter of the compound predicate in each sentence. Blacken the letter for that choice in the answer box to the right.

4. My friend studied and passed the test for his high school diploma.

   a. friend studied   b. studied and passed   c. passed the test   d. high school

   4. ⓐ ⓑ ⓒ ⓓ

5. A group of men and women pushed and pulled the car out of the mud.

   a. A group   b. men and women   c. pushed and pulled   d. car out

   5. ⓐ ⓑ ⓒ ⓓ

6. The flames waved and danced against the night sky.

   a. flames   b. flames waved   c. waved and danced   d. night sky

   6. ⓐ ⓑ ⓒ ⓓ

F Identifying
Sentences

Find the letter that tells what, if anything, is missing from each group of words. Blacken the circle for that choice in the answer box to the right.

7. Men, women, and small children.

   a. subject   b. predicate   c. comma   d. nothing

   7. ⓐ ⓑ ⓒ ⓓ

8. He read the book and took notes.

   a. subject   b. predicate   c. comma   d. nothing

   8. ⓐ ⓑ ⓒ ⓓ

9. It was getting light and birds began to sing.

   a. subject   b. predicate   c. comma   d. nothing

   9. ⓐ ⓑ ⓒ ⓓ

10. We thought he would come right home but he did not return for hours.

    a. subject   b. predicate   c. comma   d. nothing

    10. ⓐ ⓑ ⓒ ⓓ

11. Carefully washed and wiped the dishes from breakfast.

    a. subject   b. predicate   c. comma   d. nothing

    11. ⓐ ⓑ ⓒ ⓓ

Number Missed	0	1	2	3	4	5	6	7	8	9	10	11
Percent Correct	100	91	82	73	64	55	45	36	27	18	9	0

Four Kinds of Sentences

What Happened to David Lang?

On September 13, 1880, David Lang walked into an open field. He was never seen again. Lang had come out of the house with his wife. He spoke to his children about a wooden toy he had bought for them the day before. Then he started to walk across the pasture. Judge Peck and Mrs. Lang's brother drove up in a buggy. The judge saw Lang in the field and started to call to him. At that moment Lang <u>vanished</u>.

Mrs. Lang and the men were afraid that he had fallen into a hole. They raced into the field. There was no hole and no man. David Lang had <u>literally</u> vanished before their eyes. It is a <u>mystery</u> that has never been <u>solved</u>.

Read the story carefully. Study the words before and after each underlined word. They will help you understand what the underlined word means.

Building Vocabulary Circle the letter of the word or words in the box below that mean almost the same as the underlined words.

1. <u>vanished</u>	a. called out	b. blinded	c. dropped from sight	d. stood still
2. <u>literally</u>	a. hardly	b. really	c. almost	d. often
3. <u>mystery</u>	a. puzzle	b. crime	c. ending	d. lie
4. <u>solved</u>	a. forgotten	b. repeated	c. found	d. answered

Check your choices in a dictionary. Add these words and their meanings to your vocabulary notebook. Try to use them as often as you can.

There are four kinds of sentences. A **declarative** sentence tells something. It ends with a period.

• You are a good worker.

An **interrogative** sentence asks a question. It ends with a question mark.

• Are you a good worker?

An **imperative** sentence gives a command. It also ends with a period.

• Be a good worker.

An **exclamatory** sentence signals excitement. It ends with an exclamation mark.

• Watch that hammer!

Try It   Add the correct end mark to each sentence. Then tell what kind of sentence it is by writing DEC for declarative, INT for interrogative, IMP for imperative, or EXC for exclamatory. Check your answers on page 100.

1. What happened to David Lang_____

2. People were looking at him when he vanished_____

3. Tell the police what happened_____

4. What a story this is_____

This is a warm-up exercise. If you make two or more mistakes, read the definitions and examples on page 98 again before working exercise A.

A Identifying Kinds of Sentences   Add the correct end mark to each sentence. Then tell what kind of sentence it is by writing DEC for declarative, INT for interrogative, IMP for imperative, or EXC for exclamatory.

1. Scientists studied the place where Lang vanished_____ _____

2. Did they find a break beneath the pasture_____ _____

3. No, it was unbroken_____ _____

4. How strange that was_____ _____

5. Tell me why some of his servants quit afterwards_____ _____

6. They were afraid_____ _____

B Writing Imperative Sentences   Rewrite the following sentences as imperative sentences, or commands. Begin the imperative sentence with the word on the line. Be sure to use the correct end mark.

1. You should remember that the search went on for a month.

   Remember _____

2. You should realize that the grass changed where he vanished.

   Realize _____

3. Can you imagine that his cows would not eat that grass?

   Imagine _____

4. Do you understand that even insects would not live there?

   Understand _____

Remember to end each sentence with the correct punctuation mark.

Number Missed	0	1	2	3	4	5	6	7	8	9	10	11	12	13	14	15	16
Percent Correct	100	94	88	81	75	69	63	56	50	44	38	31	25	19	13	6	0

C Writing Questions

Change the following sentences into questions. Begin the question with the word on the line.

1. The Lang children were going to the pasture.

   Were _____

2. They had heard a faint cry for help.

   Had _____

3. Mrs. Lang is calling to her husband.

   Is _____

4. She did hear David Lang's voice answer.

   Did _____

Remember to end each sentence with a question mark.

D Proofreading

There are six errors in the following paragraph. Put missing punctuation marks where they belong. Cross out each other error and write the correction above it. The first error is marked for you. You should find five more.

Every day the family returned to the tall grass; They called to David Lang. Each day his voice answered, it got fainter. After a few day there was no answer. David Lang was gone. What happened to him No one knows. Some people think that he vanished into time. Others thinks that he was taken away by a UFO. Could you have solved the mistery?

You should find and correct the following errors:
- 2 missing punctuation marks
- 1 incorrect noun form
- 1 incorrect verb form
- 1 misspelled word

E Writing Sentences

Answer each question with a complete declarative sentence. If you need help, study the paragraph on page 98 and exercises A through C.

1. Where was David Lang before he vanished? _____

   _____

2. Who saw him the day he vanished? _____

   _____

3. How long did the search for Lang go on? _____

   _____

Try It Answers for page 99

1. ? INT
2. . DEC
3. . IMP
4. ! EXC

Number Missed	0	1	2	3	4	5	6	7	8	9	10	11	12
Percent Correct	100	92	83	75	67	58	50	42	33	25	17	8	0

Focus on Writing

Writing
Journal Entries

A journal is a place to record thoughts, ideas, and things that happen. Journals can be used for the writer alone, or they can be shared with other people.

Imagine that you were a neighbor of the Lang family when David Lang vanished. You keep a journal, so naturally you write about the mystery. What is written for one day is called an entry. On the lines below, write two entries that might have been in your journal. The first should be for the day David Lang disappeared. The second should be for one month later. Use the lesson if you want to review what happened. But also imagine how you felt about these events. Include your own thoughts in your entries. In the second entry, describe what you think happened to David Lang.

Do you keep a journal? If you want to begin one, just use a notebook. Remember, a journal can be used for many different things. For example, if you hear a joke you want to remember, write it in your journal!

September 13, 1880

_____

_____

_____

_____

_____

_____

October 13, 1880

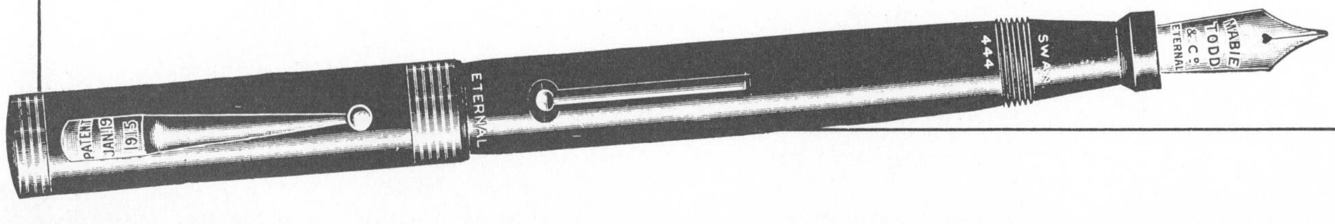

_____

_____

_____

_____

_____

_____

_____

_____

Adverb Clauses

The Underwater World

Read the story carefully. Study the words before and after each underlined word. They will help you understand what the underlined word means.

Skin divers "live" in a world that stretches beneath the surface of rivers, lakes, and oceans. In that world they take pictures, catch fish, and <u>collect</u> shells. Sometimes they even <u>locate</u> treasure!

There are two kinds of skin diving: breath-hold and scuba. Breath-hold divers simply hold their breath underwater. Scuba divers use tanks of air to help them breathe underwater. Both kinds of divers may use <u>canvas</u> or net bags to help them carry things underwater. They may also <u>employ</u> knives, underwater flashlights, waterproof cameras, and spear guns to help them explore and work in their world.

Building Vocabulary   Circle the letter of the word or words in the box below that mean almost the same as the underlined words.

1. <u>collect</u>	a. buy	b. clean	c. sell	d. gather
2. <u>locate</u>	a. explain	b. find	c. spend	d. return
3. <u>canvas</u>	a. kind of cloth	b. kind of paper	c. pocketbook	d. very dark color
4. <u>employ</u>	a. forget	b. lose	c. use	d. expect

Check your choices in a dictionary. Add these words and their meanings to your vocabulary notebook. Try to use them as often as you can.

A **clause** is a group of words that is part of a sentence, but that cannot stand alone as a sentence. An **adverb clause** begins with a connecting word such as <u>when</u>, <u>if</u>, <u>after</u>, <u>before</u>, <u>because</u>, <u>since</u>, or <u>until</u>. It modifies the words that do stand alone as a sentence. An adverb clause often explains when, why, or under what conditions something happens.

- I might dive **after I learn more about it**. (tells when)

- Skin diving should be fun **because I like to swim**. (tells why)

- Divers can drown **if they make mistakes**. (tells under what conditions)

When an adverb clause begins a sentence, it is set off by a comma.

- **After I learn more about it,** I might dive.

- **If they make mistakes,** divers can drown.

Try It

Underline the adverb clause in each sentence. Circle the connecting word that begins each adverb clause. Check your answers on page 104.

1. Swimmers explore another world when they skin dive.

2. Divers without tanks hold their breath until they surface.

3. Since scuba was invented, some divers stay down longer.

4. They can breathe underwater because they carry air tanks.

This is a warm-up exercise. If you make two or more mistakes, read the definitions and examples on page 102 before working exercise A.

A Identifying Adverb Clauses

Underline the adverb clause in each sentence. Circle the connecting word that begins the adverb clause.

1. You will need certain things if you want to skin dive.

2. Because you need to see well, you will use a face mask.

3. You will breathe with your face in the water when you use a snorkel.

4. Until you put on swim fins, swimming may tire you out.

5. You may enjoy swimming more after you get into a wet suit.

6. When you swim, water gets inside the wet suit.

7. The water becomes warm because your body heats it.

Notice that when the adverb clause comes at the beginning of the sentence, it is separated from the rest of the sentence by a comma.

B Writing Adverb Clauses

Use one of the adverb clauses in the box to complete each sentence.

old diving suit

until they are done or need air	when divers want to come up
if they want to stay underwater	since they come up often for air

1. _____

_____ divers must wear belts with weights in them.

2. Skin divers stay underwater _____

_____

3. _____ air-filled vests

will float them to the surface.

4. Breath-hold divers cannot go too deep _____

_____

Remember to capitalize the first word in each sentence and to end each sentence with a period. If the adverb clause begins the sentence, use a comma to separate it from the rest of the sentence.

Number Missed	0	1	2	3	4	5	6	7	8	9	10	11	12	13	14	15	16	17	18
Percent Correct	100	94	89	83	78	72	67	61	56	50	44	39	33	28	22	17	11	6	0

C Writing Sentences with Adverb Clauses

Combine each of the following pairs of sentences into a single sentence. Use the connecting word in parentheses to create an adverb clause within the sentence. The first one is done for you.

You may place the adverb clause at the beginning or the end of a sentence. If it begins the sentence, remember to set if off with a comma.

Remember to begin each sentence with a capital letter. End each sentence with a period.

1. The water is so clear. Some areas are perfect for diving.   (**because**)

   Some areas are perfect for diving because the water is so clear. OR

   Because the water is so clear, some areas are perfect for diving.

2. Scuba diving is dangerous. You must take lessons.   (**since**)

   _____

   _____

3. Deep dives can be deadly. You don't know what you're doing.   (**when**)

   _____

   _____

4. Your lungs can burst. You surface faster than your air bubbles.   (**if**)

   _____

   _____

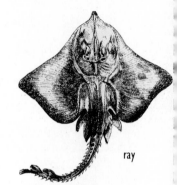

ray

D Proofreading

Find and correct the errors in the following paragraph. Put punctuation marks where they belong. Then cross out each error and write the correction above it. There are six errors. The first one is marked for you. You should find and correct the following five errors:

- 1 missing comma
- 1 missing end punctuation mark
- 1 word that should be capitalized
- 1 incorrect verb form
- 1 misspelled word

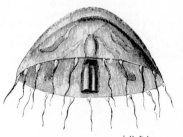

jellyfish

Many people use scuba diving in their work. Some scuba divers repair~~repairs~~ ships. When some scuba divers dive they find things on the ocean floor. Other divers help build, check, and repair bridges. some scientists use scuba diving to study fish and underwater plants. Others studies shells and rocks at the bottom of rivers, lakes, and oceans. For some, scuba diving may be an intresting sport For others, it may be the everyday world of work.

Try It Answers for page 103

1. (when) they skin dive
2. (until) they surface
3. (Since) scuba was invented
4. (because) they carry air tanks.

Number Missed	0	1	2	3	4	5	6	7	8
Percent Correct	100	88	75	63	50	38	25	13	0

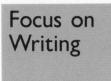

Focus on Writing

Writing a List

Skin divers must be prepared. They need special equipment for their underwater exploring. For scuba divers, being prepared is a matter of life and breath!

Imagine that you are preparing for a weekend on an island. You and one friend will row to the island in a small boat. It is in the middle of a lake and has trees and bushes on it. The weather is warm. The clear, clean water is filled with fish. There is a cabin on the island. It has two cots in it. There are also things like pots and dishes. There is, however, no electricity.

On the lines below, write a list of things you will take to the island. Try to be prepared for whatever happens. For example, what if it rains? Plan what you will need for two days, rain or shine. Think about food, clothes, and supplies. Remember, your boat is small. And there will be two of you in it!

Adjective Clauses with That

Making Lemonade

As one saying goes, "When life hands you a lemon, make lemonade." That's what Bill Cosby did. He turned <u>adversity</u> into <u>success</u>. His father left the family when he was young. One brother died. To help his family, Bill took care of his younger brother. He also earned money by working after school in a store. Then he dropped out of high school rather than repeat the tenth grade.

Yet Bill Cosby <u>persevered</u>. He returned to school and went on to earn an advanced <u>degree</u> from the University of Massachusetts. He became a successful comedian, actor, writer, and producer. Today, his hit TV program *The Cosby Show* is enjoyed and admired by millions of viewers.

Read the story carefully. Study the words before and after each underlined word. They will help you understand what the underlined word means.

Building Vocabulary Circle the letter of the word or words in the box below that mean almost the same as the underlined words.

1. <u>adversity</u>	a. hardship	b. TV ad	c. sour fruit	d. work
2. <u>success</u>	a. business	b. victory	c. bad luck	d. comedy
3. <u>persevered</u>	a. waited	b. escaped	c. kept trying	d. kept failing
4. <u>degree</u>	a. job training		c. serious illness	
	b. grade showing lack of effort		d. title given for completing a study program	

Check your choices in a dictionary. Add these words and their meanings to your vocabulary notebook. Try to use them as often as you can.

An **adjective clause** is a part of some sentences, but it cannot stand alone as a sentence. It modifies a noun in the sentence it is part of. It often begins with the word <u>that</u>. <u>That</u> is a **relative pronoun**. It relates, or connects, the adjective clause to the sentence.

- This is a story **that interests me**. (modifies <u>story</u>)

- The life **that he has** is good. (modifies <u>life</u>)

- Shows **that include comedy** are nice to watch. (modifies <u>Shows</u>)

Like other pronouns, relative pronouns are related to a noun. The noun to which this relative pronoun is related is called its antecedent. Notice that in the example sentences above the pronoun <u>that</u> is related to each of the nouns it modifies.

Other relative pronouns are <u>which</u> and <u>who</u>. You will study adjective clauses that begin with these relative pronouns in Lessons 24 and 25.

Try It

Underline the adjective clause in each sentence. Circle the word that it modifies. Check your answers on page 108.

1. Bill Cosby came from a family that was full of love.

2. The many chores that Bill did helped his family.

3. Bill dropped out of a school that wanted him to repeat a grade.

4. He joined the Navy, but it was not a life that he liked.

This is a warm-up exercise. If you make two or more mistakes, read the definitions and examples on page 106 again before working exercise A.

A Identifying Adjective Clauses

Underline the adjective clause in each sentence. Circle the word the clause modifies.

1. While in the Navy, Cosby earned the high school diploma that he needed.

2. Later, he went to college on a scholarship that he received for sports.

3. The sports that he played were football and track.

4. The subjects that he studied were science and physical education.

5. Being a doctor or teacher was an idea that interested him.

6. Then Cosby discovered the fact that he could make people laugh.

7. He told stories that people found funny.

8. He was the first black actor to star in a TV show that was seen nationwide.

9. The TV series that he starred in was called *I Spy.*

Notice that adjective clauses may come at the end or in the middle of a sentence. Adjective clauses always come right after the nouns that they modify. In addition to a subject and predicate, the clause often includes other words.

B Writing Adjective Clauses

Complete each sentence with an adjective clause from the box below.

The Cosby Show cast

that helps people learn	that now bears his name
that he had postponed	that he earned

1. Cosby wanted to finish the education _____.

2. With the advanced degree _____, Cosby could have become a college professor.

3. Instead, he created a show _____ about handling real-life problems with love, hard work, and humor.

4. The hit program _____ is *The Cosby Show.*

Complete the sentences you are sure of first. Cross out each clause as you use it. Then go back to the sentences you left blank. See if you can find the correct clauses left on the list.

Number Missed	0	1	2	3	4	5	6	7	8	9	10	11	12	13	14	15	16	17	18	19	20	21	22
Percent Correct	100	95	91	86	82	77	73	68	64	59	55	50	45	41	36	32	27	23	18	14	9	5	0

Lesson 23 Part 3 Adjective Clauses with That ■■■■■■■■■■■■■

C Writing Adjective Clauses

Use your own words to complete the adjective clause in each of the following sentences. Be sure that each adjective clause has both a subject and a predicate.

1. Bill Cosby came from a family that _____

_____

2. He went to a high school that _____

_____

3. While he was in the Navy, Cosby earned the high school diploma that ___

_____

4. The jokes and stories that _____
made many people laugh.

Any adjective clause that makes sense in the sentence is correct.

D Proofreading

Find and correct the errors in the following paragraph. Put punctuation marks where they belong. Cross out each error. Write the correction above it. There are six errors. The first is marked for you. You should find five more.

       Cosby's
Most of Bill ~~Cosbys~~ stories make people learn as well as laugh. Cosby think of himself as a teacher as well as an acter. he has been on many TV programs that teach childs to read and write He takes time to help those who need help.

You should find and correct the following errors:
- 1 missing punctuation mark
- 1 incorrect verb form
- 1 incorrect noun form
- 1 word that needs to be capitalized
- 1 misspelled word

E Writing Sentences

Answer the following questions. Each answer should include an adjective clause that begins with that.

1. What was one problem that Cosby had when he was young? _____

_____

2. What two subjects did Cosby study in college? _____

_____

3. What kinds of TV programs does Cosby appear on? _____

_____

4. What good thing happened to Cosby in the Navy? _____

_____

Try It Answers for page 107

1. family that was full of love
2. chores that Bill did
3. school that wanted him to repeat a grade
4. life that he liked

Number Missed	0	1	2	3	4	5	6	7	8	9	10	11	12	13
Percent Correct	100	92	85	77	69	62	54	46	38	31	23	15	8	0

108

Focus on Writing

Writing a Paragraph

Bill Cosby has appeared in one of the most popular shows on television. Imagine that you have been asked to plan a television show. First, you have to decide what kind of show it will be. For example, it could be a comedy, an adventure story, a detective story, or a soap opera. It might be a cartoon. Think about different kinds of shows and choose one. Then write a paragraph telling what your show will be like. Include in your paragraph the answer to each question below.

- What kind of show will it be?
- What will the name of it be?
- Who will the main characters be?
- Where will the story take place?
- What is the basic story line?
- Who will star in the show?

Adjective Clauses with Which

The Puzzle of the Pyramids

The kings of Egypt (EE jipt) built pyramids more than 4,500 years ago. These wonderful structures are made of stone blocks. Some blocks weigh as much as five tons. The blocks of one pyramid fit so <u>snugly</u> that a piece of paper cannot be slipped between them. The huge blocks were cut from <u>solid</u> stone. They were then probably floated down the Nile River on rafts and dragged into place on sleds and rollers. It would have taken hundreds of thousands of workers more than 20 years to <u>construct</u> a pyramid.

Read the story carefully. Study the words before and after each underlined word. They will help you understand what the underlined word means.

Building Vocabulary   Circle the letter of the word or words in the box below that mean almost the same as the underlined words.

1. <u>structures</u>	a. doors	b. writings	c. plans	d. buildings
2. <u>snugly</u>	a. tightly	b. carelessly	c. loosely	d. poorly
3. <u>solid</u>	a. crashed	b. not hollow	c. broken	d. poorly
4. <u>construct</u>	a. build	b. plan	c. decorate	d. take apart

Check your choices in a dictionary. Add these words and their meanings to your vocabulary notebook. Try to use them as often as you can.

In Lesson 23 you learned that an adjective clause is a part of a sentence. It modifies a noun or a pronoun. Some adjective clauses begin with the relative pronoun <u>that</u>. Others begin with the relative pronoun <u>which</u>. Which is used when the clause gives some extra information about the noun that the clause modifies. Clauses that give extra information are called **non-essential clauses**.

Commas are used to separate an adjective clause that begins with <u>which</u> from the rest of the sentence. If the clause comes at the end of the sentence, one comma is needed.

Remember, a relative pronoun relates or connects the clause it begins to the main part of the sentence. The pronoun takes the place of the noun that it modifies.

- The pyramids are constructed of huge stone blocks, **which were cut from solid stone**.

Two commas are needed if the clause comes in the middle of the sentence.

- The blocks, **which weigh up to five tons,** were cut by hundreds of workers.

Adjective clauses that begin with <u>that</u> are never set off with commas.

Try It | Underline the adjective clause in each sentence. Circle the word that the clause modifies. Check your answers on page 112.

1. Pyramids, which are places where kings were buried, are still standing.

2. Rafts, which floated down the Nile, may have carried the stone blocks.

3. Workers pulled the blocks on rollers, which were made of logs.

This is a warm-up exercise. If you make one or more mistakes, read the definitions and examples on page 110 again before working exercise A.

A Identifying Adjective Clauses | Underline each adjective clause. Circle the word that the clause modifies.

1. The first pyramid, which was built in 2650 B.C., has rough sides.

2. That structure, which has sides like steps, is called a step pyramid.

3. Other pyramids, which were built the same way, have smooth sides.

4. The base of one pyramid, which is called the Great Pyramid, is larger than ten football fields.

5. It has more than two million blocks, which average 2½ tons each.

6. It has lost some stones from its top, which was once 481 feet tall.

7. One room, which is smaller than the king's room, held the queen's body.

Notice how commas are used to set off adjective clauses that give extra information about the nouns they modify.

B Writing Adjective Clauses | Complete each sentence with an adjective clause from the box below.

| which slope upward | which a king could use in the "next life" |
| which was smaller than the king's | which were built to protect their bodies |

1. Kings were buried in pyramids, _____

_____ .

2. Gold and jewels, _____

_____ , were buried with him.

3. The sides of the pyramid, _____

_____ , were built to help his soul climb to the gods.

4. Sometimes a queen was buried in a separate room, _____

_____ .

Complete the sentences you are sure of first. Cross out each clause as you use it. Then go back to the sentences that you left blank. See if you can find the correct clauses left on the list.

Number Missed	0	1	2	3	4	5	6	7	8	9	10	11	12	13	14	15	16	17	18
Percent Correct	100	94	89	83	78	72	67	61	56	50	44	39	33	28	22	17	11	6	0

C Writing
Adjective Clauses

Use your own words to complete each adjective clause in the following sentences. Use the information you have learned in this lesson to complete the sentences. If you need help, look again at the story on page 110 and at exercise A.

1. Pyramids, which _____,
   were made of stone blocks.

2. A step pyramid, which _____,
   has rough sides.

3. Building a pyramid was a hard job, which _____

   _____

4. The blocks for pyramids were probably carried on rafts, which _____

   _____

5. The blocks, which _____,
   may then have been dragged into place on sleds and rollers.

6. There was a king's room, which _____

   _____

7. No one really knows how the pyramids, which _____

   _____ were built.

D Proofreading

There are six errors in the following paragraph. Put missing punctuation marks where they belong. Cross out each error and write the correction above it. The first one is done for you. You should find and correct the following five errors:

- 1 word that should be capitalized
- 1 incorrect verb form
- 1 misspelled word
- 1 missing end punctuation mark
- 1 missing comma

Some people do not believe the pyramids were built by workers from
Egypt
~~egypt~~. Some think they were built by people from Atlantis which is a land

that may have vanished into the Atlantic ocean. Others think the pyramids

were built by people from space. One person say there is only one way to

explane how the heavy blocks were lifted into place. He says a UFO did it.

How do you think they were lifted

**Try It Answers
for page 111**

1. (Pyramids,) which
   are places where
   kings were
   buried,

2. (Rafts,) which
   floated down the
   Nile,

3. (rollers) which
   were made of
   logs.

Number Missed	0	1	2	3	4	5	6	7	8	9	10	11	12
Percent Correct	100	92	83	75	67	58	50	42	33	25	17	8	0

Focus on Writing

Writing a
Descriptive
Paragraph

The pyramids are not only strong structures that have lasted 4500 years. They have simple, clean lines that are pleasing to the eye. Think how much careful planning was needed before even one stone was cut!

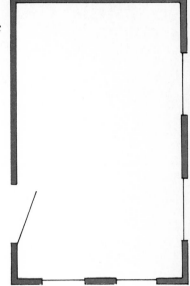

Imagine that you have been given one room in a house to plan. You may decorate the room any way you like. On the lines below, write a paragraph telling how the room will look. Before you begin writing, think about each question below.

• What will the room be used for?
• Will it have windows? If so, will you use window coverings?
• What kind of floor will the room have?
• What will be in the room? Furniture? Bookcases? Games? A stereo or television?
• What colors will you use in the room?
• What, if anything, will be on the walls?

Now, plan a room you would enjoy using!

Describe the size, color, and shape of things in the room very carefully and in detail.

Adjective Clauses with <u>Who</u>

Oscar

Each year the Academy Awards <u>acknowledge</u> the best in films. The best picture, the best actors, and the best workers behind the scenes are honored. Each winner is given a statue. The statue stands 10 inches tall, weighs seven pounds, and is covered with gold. It is known as an Oscar. How did it get that name?

The Academy of Motion Picture Arts and Sciences <u>bestows</u> the awards. In 1931, a person who worked for the Academy saw one of the statues and said, "Why that looks just like my Uncle Oscar!" The name stuck.

Oscar may not be very <u>massive</u>, but he is a very <u>significant</u> figure to those who work in the motion picture industry.

Read the story carefully. Study the words before and after each underlined word. They will help you understand what the underlined word means.

Building Vocabulary   Circle the letter of the word or words in the box below that mean almost the same as the underlined words.

1. <u>acknowledge</u>	a. desire	b. deliver	c. recognize	d. pay
2. <u>bestows</u>	a. changes	b. gives	c. loans	d. loses
3. <u>massive</u>	a. large	b. tiny	c. happy	d. difficult
4. <u>significant</u>	a. useless	b. foolish	c. expensive	d. important

Check your choices in a dictionary. Add these words and their meanings to your vocabulary notebook. Try to use them as often as you can.

Adjective clauses can also begin with the relative pronoun <u>who</u>. The relative pronoun links the clause to a noun or pronoun in the main part of the sentence. The relative pronoun <u>who</u> always modifies a noun or pronoun in the main part of the sentence that names a person or people.

Commas are sometimes used to separate an adjective clause that begins with <u>who</u> from the rest of the sentence. Commas are used when the clause gives extra information about the noun or pronoun that the clause modifies.

Humphrey Bogart

- Humphrey Bogart, **who starred in many films,** won an Oscar for his performance in *The African Queen.* (modifies <u>Humphrey Bogart</u>)

No commas are used when the adjective clause gives needed information.

- Those individuals **who win an Oscar** should be proud. (modifies <u>individuals</u>)

Try It

Underline each adjective clause in the following sentences. Circle the word that the clause modifies. Check your answers on page 116.

1. Paul Newman and Burt Lancaster, who play main parts, are called leading actors.

2. Supporting actors are people who play less important roles.

3. People who direct films also win awards.

This is a warm-up exercise. If you make one or more mistakes, read the definitions and examples on page 114 again before working exercise A.

A Identifying Adjective Clauses

Underline each adjective clause. Circle the word that the clause modifies.

1. A woman who worked in the Academy library named the award for her uncle.

2. Robert Redford, who won the award for Best Director, received his Oscar in 1981.

3. In 1982 the Best Actress was Meryl Streep, who starred in *Sophie's Choice*.

4. A Best Supporting Actor was Jack Nicholson, who won the award in 1983.

5. The 1987 awards included some presenters who did unusual things.

6. One person who gave out awards looked like Bugs Bunny.

Notice that adjective clauses include words other than the subject and the verb.

Meryl Streep

B Writing Adjective Clauses

Choose an adjective clause from the box below to complete each sentence.

who played a supporting part in *Hannah and Her Sisters*
who is a deaf woman
who directed *Platoon*
who played the leading role in *The Color of Money*

1. Best Actor was won by Paul Newman, _____

_____ .

2. Best Supporting Actor went to Michael Caine, _____

_____ .

3. Marlee Matlin, _____

_____ , used sign language to accept the Best Actress award.

4. Best Director went to Oliver Stone, _____ .

Complete the sentences you are sure of first. Cross out each clause as you use it. Then go back to the sentences that you left blank. See if you can find the correct clauses left on the list.

Number Missed	0	1	2	3	4	5	6	7	8	9	10	11	12	13	14	15	16
Percent Correct	100	94	88	81	75	69	63	56	50	44	38	31	25	19	13	6	0

Lesson 25   Part 3   Adjective Clauses with <u>Who</u>   ■ ■ ■ ■ ■ ■ ■ ■ ■ ■ ■

C Writing Sentences with Adjective Clauses

Use the relative pronoun <u>who</u> to turn one sentence in each pair below into an adjective clause. Then write the pair of sentences as a single sentence. Use commas where they are needed. Study the example below.

- Movie stars are not always good actors.
  Movie stars make a lot of money.

- Movie stars **who make a lot of money** are not always good actors. <u>OR</u>
  Movie stars, **who are not always good actors,** make a lot of money.

1. Ruby Dee is a superb actress. Ruby Dee stars in many films.

   _____

   _____

   _____

2. Experts work behind the scenes. Experts are vital to the film industry.

   _____

   _____

3. A good actor cares about quality. A good actor may refuse a part.

   _____

   _____

Notice that either sentence in each pair can be turned into an adjective clause. In the example, the first adjective clause is not separated from the rest of the sentence by commas. The clause gives needed information about movie stars.

Sally Field and Dustin Hoffman

D Proofreading

There are six errors in the following paragraph. Put missing punctuation marks where they belong. Cross out each error and write the correction above it. The first one is done for you. You should find and correct the following errors:

- 1 missing punctuation mark
- 1 incorrect noun form
- 1 word that should be capitalized
- 2 misspelled words

Each week ~~millions~~ millions of people go to theaters to see films. Countless others watch films on TV. The making of films, or movies, is big busines It takes much money, time, and work to make a movie. Peoples must write the script. People are also needed to produce, direct, and film it. good actors and actresses must play in it. Sometimes hundreds of people who are called extras are hired to apear in the film.

Try It Answers for page 115

1. Paul Newman and Burt Lancaster, who play main parts,
2. people who play less important roles
3. People who direct films

Number Missed	0	1	2	3	4	5	6	7	8
Percent Correct	100	88	75	63	50	38	25	13	0

116

Focus on Writing

Writing
Ad Copy

This is a movie ad that might be in a newspaper.

Plan an ad like the one for *Spaceship Mars.* Use a movie you have seen in a theater or on television. Or, make up a name for a movie. On the lines below, write the copy, or words, you will use in the ad.

Remember to use adjectives to describe the movie.

_____

_____

_____

_____

_____

_____

_____

Use a separate piece of paper and design your ad. Use pictures and other details to show how the ad would look.

A Identifying Kinds of Sentences

Add the correct end mark to each sentence. Then tell what kind of sentence it is by writing DEC for declarative, IMP for imperative, INT for interrogative, or EXC for exclamatory. For help, review page 98.

1. Did you buy a new pair of shoes____ _____

2. Buy a new pair of shoes____ _____

3. You will buy a new pair of shoes____ _____

4. It is warm for this time of year____ _____

5. We trained our dog not to chase cars____ _____

6. Write your address and telephone number on this paper____ _____

7. What time do you have to go to work tomorrow____ _____

8. What a nice jacket that is____ _____

9. Tell Fang to stop barking____ _____

10. Their telephone number is not listed____ _____

11. Why does it always rain on Saturday and Sunday____ _____

12. Be very careful____ _____

B Identifying Adverb Clauses

Read the sentences below. Underline each adverb clause. Circle the connecting word that begins the clause. For help, review page 102.

1. We will stop when we get tired.

2. I will call her if I do not have a chance to write.

3. Heather was tired after she ran so far.

4. Yesterday he was late because he missed his bus.

5. I have not seen her since she left the office.

6. Most children are not ready to walk until they can crawl.

7. She calls my sister every day after school is over.

8. The game cannot be played until the rain stops.

9. Please let me know if the telephone rings.

10. The grass has grown three inches since it was cut last.

Number Missed	0	1	2	3	4	5	6	7	8	9	10	11	12	13	14	15	16	17	18	19	20	21	22	23	24
Percent Correct	100	98	95	93	91	89	86	84	82	80	77	75	73	70	68	66	64	61	59	57	55	52	50	48	45

Number Missed	25	26	27	28	29	30	31	32	33	34	35	36	37	38	39	40	41	42	43	44
Percent Correct	43	41	39	36	34	32	30	27	25	23	20	18	16	14	11	9	7	5	2	0

C Identifying Adjective Clauses with **That**

Underline the adjective clause in each sentence. Circle the word that the clause modifies. For help, review page 106.

1. Maria works at a job that she likes very much.

2. Where is the suit that you want me to take to the cleaners?

3. The music that he enjoys is very loud.

4. Please pay for the book that you lost.

5. The room that you are in is the living room.

6. We all played the game that she got for her birthday.

7. The friends that you make are important.

8. Is this the cat that climbed to the top of the maple tree?

D Identifying Adjective Clauses with **Which**

Underline the adjective clause in each of the following sentences. Circle the word that the clause modifies. For help, review page 110.

1. My tools, which are in the garage, are hanging on pegs.

2. I came by way of School Street, which is being repaired.

3. The directions, which she gave us, are very clear.

4. We visited the Sears Tower, which is the world's tallest building.

5. I am lost without my watch, which I forgot to wear this morning.

6. The fire, which started in the night, spread to other buildings.

E Identifying Adjective Clauses with **Who**

Underline the adjective clause in each sentence. Circle the word that the clause modifies. For help, review page 114.

1. I have an uncle who works at the airport.

2. People who are true friends will always stand by you.

3. My aunt, who is my mother's sister, has a beautiful voice.

4. People who run a high fever should see a doctor.

5. The man with the cane is Mr. Perez, who lives next door to me.

6. Men and women who work in libraries usually like books.

Number Missed	0	1	2	3	4	5	6	7	8	9	10	11	12	13	14	15	16	17	18	19	20	21	22	23	24
Percent Correct	100	98	95	93	90	88	85	83	80	78	75	73	70	68	65	63	60	58	55	53	50	48	45	43	40

Number Missed	25	26	27	28	29	30	31	32	33	34	35	36	37	38	39	40
Percent Correct	38	35	33	30	28	25	23	20	18	15	13	10	8	5	3	0

Practice Test: Lessons 21–25 Part I ■■■■■■■■■■■■■■■■

A Kinds of Sentences Find the letter of the word that names each sentence. Blacken the circle of that letter in the answer box to the right.

1. I hope that it does not rain tomorrow.
   a. declarative   b. interrogative   c. imperative   d. exclamatory   **1.** ⓐ ⓑ ⓒ ⓓ

2. Let me tell you a true story.
   a. declarative   b. interrogative   c. imperative   d. exclamatory   **2.** ⓐ ⓑ ⓒ ⓓ

3. I am going to see Paula in a play next week.
   a. declarative   b. interrogative   c. imperative   d. exclamatory   **3.** ⓐ ⓑ ⓒ ⓓ

4. What an amazing photograph that is, Grandmother!
   a. declarative   b. interrogative   c. imperative   d. exclamatory   **4.** ⓐ ⓑ ⓒ ⓓ

5. Is it cheaper to go by train, plane, or bus?
   a. declarative   b. interrogative   c. imperative   d. exclamatory   **5.** ⓐ ⓑ ⓒ ⓓ

B Adverb Clauses Find the letter of the word that begins the adverb clause in each sentence. Then blacken the circle of that letter in the answer box to the right.

6. I will go to the play with her if she asks me.
   a. I   b. to   c. with   d. if   **6.** ⓐ ⓑ ⓒ ⓓ

7. It will be cold until the sun is higher in the sky.
   a. It   b. until   c. is   d. in   **7.** ⓐ ⓑ ⓒ ⓓ

8. I went to the dentist because I needed to have my teeth checked.
   a. to   b. because   c. needed   d. my   **8.** ⓐ ⓑ ⓒ ⓓ

9. I have not seen the cat since you put it out last night.
   a. I   b. seen   c. since   d. out   **9.** ⓐ ⓑ ⓒ ⓓ

10. I will pick you up with the car this afternoon when I go shopping.
    a. will   b. up   c. with   d. when   **10.** ⓐ ⓑ ⓒ ⓓ

11. Don't forget to brush your teeth each time after you eat.
    a. forget   b. to   c. each   d. after   **11.** ⓐ ⓑ ⓒ ⓓ

12. I do not think we should go out until it stops raining.
    a. I   b. do   c. out   d. until   **12.** ⓐ ⓑ ⓒ ⓓ

13. You will never be able to do anything well if you don't keep trying.
    a. be   b. to   c. if   d. you   **13.** ⓐ ⓑ ⓒ ⓓ

14. Come quickly when you hear me call to you.
    a. Come   b. when   c. you   d. to   **14.** ⓐ ⓑ ⓒ ⓓ

Number Missed	0	1	2	3	4	5	6	7	8	9	10	11	12	13	14
Percent Correct	100	93	86	79	71	64	57	50	43	36	29	21	14	7	0

C Adjective Clauses

Find the letter of the word in each sentence that the adjective clause modifies. Then blacken the circle of that letter in the answer box to the right.

Answer Box

1. This is the house that Jack built.
   a. This   b. house   c. Jack   d. built

   1. ⓐ ⓑ ⓒ ⓓ

2. Aunt Rose was shocked at the broken vase, which the dog knocked over.
   a. Aunt Rose   b. shocked   c. vase   d. which

   2. ⓐ ⓑ ⓒ ⓓ

3. The birdhouse, which my friend made, was hanging in the oak tree.
   a. birdhouse   b. which   c. friend   d. tree

   3. ⓐ ⓑ ⓒ ⓓ

4. There are too many people in this country who are without homes.
   a. people   b. country   c. who   d. are

   4. ⓐ ⓑ ⓒ ⓓ

5. The story that he told was funny.
   a. story   b. that   c. he   d. funny

   5. ⓐ ⓑ ⓒ ⓓ

6. This is the plan that I have come up with.
   a. this   b. plan   c. that   d. come

   6. ⓐ ⓑ ⓒ ⓓ

7. George Washington, who served as our first President, was honest.
   a. George Washington   b. who   c. served   d. was

   7. ⓐ ⓑ ⓒ ⓓ

8. The Wentworth School, which is near my house, has over 300 pupils.
   a. Wentworth School   b. which   c. house   d. pupils

   8. ⓐ ⓑ ⓒ ⓓ

9. I am working for W. Duboise, which is a downtown store.
   a. I   b. W. Duboise   c. which   d. store

   9. ⓐ ⓑ ⓒ ⓓ

10. There is no reason why the law is broken by people who know better.
    a. is   b. is broken   c. people   d. know

    10. ⓐ ⓑ ⓒ ⓓ

11. I just finished reading this book, which is very interesting.
    a. I   b. book   c. which   d. interesting

    11. ⓐ ⓑ ⓒ ⓓ

12. The boys who are good players will teach the others how to play.
    a. boys   b. players   c. will teach   d. play

    12. ⓐ ⓑ ⓒ ⓓ

13. One who was lost has been found.
    a. One   b. who   c. was   d. has been

    13. ⓐ ⓑ ⓒ ⓓ

14. His car looks new, but it is one that he bought from another owner.
    a. car   b. one   c. that   d. he

    14. ⓐ ⓑ ⓒ ⓓ

15. Donna showed us the camera that her father gave her.
    a. Donna   b. showed   c. camera   d. father

    15. ⓐ ⓑ ⓒ ⓓ

16. The actors who tried out for roles were nervous.
    a. roles   b. who   c. nervous   d. actors

    16. ⓐ ⓑ ⓒ ⓓ

Number Missed	0	1	2	3	4	5	6	7	8	9	10	11	12	13	14	15	16
Percent Correct	100	94	88	81	75	69	63	56	50	44	38	31	25	19	13	6	0

Capital Letters

Where Is Flight 19?

There was nothing <u>unusual</u> about Flight 19 at first. It was <u>composed</u> of five Navy planes from Fort Lauderdale, Florida. One plane carried two men. The others each had three persons aboard. At first, the flight seemed to go according to plan. Nothing the crew said or did was unusual. Later, the base received a strange message from the flight commander. He said that they were lost and couldn't tell the direction in which they were flying. Everything looked <u>weird</u> and odd. They were never heard from again. A plane went up to search for them. It also disappeared. Many ships and planes searched for the missing flight. Years later, the Navy spent over $5 million searching the ocean floor. Not a single plane was ever <u>recovered</u>.

What happened to Flight 19? To this day, no one knows.

Read the story carefully. Study the words before and after each underlined word. They will help you understand what the underlined word means.

Building Vocabulary Circle the letter of the word or words in the box below that mean almost the same as the underlined words.

1. <u>unusual</u>	a. strange	b. long	c. short	d. sharp
2. <u>composed</u>	a. counted	b. made up	c. invented	d. designed
3. <u>weird</u>	a. expensive	b. cheap	c. strange	d. pale
4. <u>recovered</u>	a. expected	b. returned	c. found	d. changed

Check your choices in a dictionary. Add these words and their meanings to your vocabulary notebook. Try to use them as often as you can.

Begin each of the following kinds of words with a capital letter.

- The first word of a sentence: **Learn** how to use capital letters.

- The first word of a quotation: She said, "**Tell** me the answer."

- The pronoun I̲: It was not **I** who spoke.

- Proper nouns: **Timothy Wiggins**, **Fifth Avenue**

- Proper adjectives: **South American oil**

- Abbreviations for peoples' titles: **Dr.**, **Ms.**, **Mrs.**, **Mr.**, **Lt.**

- The first, last, and all important words in a title: ***The Long Way Home***

Try It

Underline each word in the sentences below that should begin with a capital letter. Check your answers on page 124.

1. The place where Flight 19 disappeared is known as the bermuda Triangle.

2. The Bermuda Triangle is off the coast of florida.

3. The commander of Flight 19 reported, "we seem to be lost."

4. since that time, ships as well as other planes have disappeared there.

This is a warm-up exercise. If you make two or more mistakes, read the definitions and examples on page 122 again before working exercise A.

A Identifying Capital Letters

Underline each word in the sentences below that should begin with a capital letter.

1. In 1965–1966, the National bureau of Standards studied the Triangle.

2. since 1854, more than 50 ships and planes have vanished there.

3. The first american ship disappeared there in March of 1918.

4. That ship was the *USS cyclops*.

5. In 1967, the United states Navy searched for Flight 19 with submarines.

6. My brother and i composed stories about what happened.

7. In 1975, the book *The Bermuda Triangle mystery—Solved* came out.

8. The book was written by lawrence D. Kusche, a research librarian.

If you need help, review the rules on page 122.

U.S.S. Cyclops

B Writing Capital Letters

Copy each group of words. Add capital letters where they are needed. You should use 24 capital letters.

1. united states navy airplane _____

2. a flyer, lt. jeffrey brown _____

3. at 116 maple drive, boston _____

4. ms. ling and i _____

5. dr. and mrs. walters _____

6. sears tower in chicago _____

7. the ship *golden fleece* from salem _____

8. john said, "you know i mean it." _____

Three words should be capitalized in each numbered item.

Number Missed	0	1	2	3	4	5	6	7	8	9	10	11	12	13	14	15	16	17	18	19	20	21	22	23	24	25	26	27	28	29	30	31	32
Percent Correct	100	97	94	91	88	84	81	78	75	72	69	66	63	59	56	53	50	47	44	41	38	34	31	28	25	22	19	16	13	9	6	3	0

C Writing
Capital Letters

On the line below each sentence, write those words that should be capitalized but were not.

1. You might want to read *the Bermuda triangle.*

_____

2. That book was written by charles berlitz.

_____

3. some people think the ocean produced a gas that confused the fliers.

_____

4. Others think the U.S. navy's flight 19 passed into another time.

_____

5. Many people think the 14 navy men were lost in the deep atlantic ocean.

_____

If you need help, review the rules on page 122. Each sentence has at least one word that should be capitalized.

D Proofreading

There are six errors in the following paragraph. Put missing punctuation marks where they belong. Cross out other errors and write the corrections above them. The first one has been done for you. You should find five more.

ideas
People have many ~~idea~~ about what happened to Flight 19. Scientists in

germany have found laughing gas in the ocean They think the gas could

make the fliers lose there way. Some peple think the fliers were caught by

sea creatures. Others thinks they slipped into another time.

You should find and correct the following errors:
- 1 word that should be capitalized
- 1 missing punctuation mark
- 1 incorrect verb form
- 2 misspelled words

E Writing
Sentences

Answer each question in a complete sentence. If you need help, look again at the story on page 122 and at exercises A and B.

1. Have many ships and planes been lost in the Bermuda Triangle? _____

_____

2. Where is the Bermuda Triangle? _____

_____

3. What was the *USS Cyclops?* _____

_____

Try It Answers for page 123

1. bermuda
2. florida
3. we
4. since

Number Missed	0	1	2	3	4	5	6	7	8	9	10	11	12	13	14	15	16	17	18
Percent Correct	100	94	89	83	78	72	67	61	56	50	44	39	33	28	22	17	11	6	0

Focus on Writing

Writing a Telephone List

What do you do when something unusual happens? When Flight 19 disappeared, planes and ships went out to search for it. In your own home, when things happen that you do not expect, you often need to get help at once. There might be an accident. All of the lights might go out. Perhaps you need to call a taxi to take you somewhere. To get the help you need, keep a list of telephone numbers by your phone. This example includes some of the places you might need to call.

Police	911
Fire	911
Ambulance	911
Poison Center	555-2232
Doctor	555-4232
Hospital	555-6865

Water Department	555-7035
Electric Company	555-9102
Gas Company	555-0031
Blue Taxi Company	555-8753
Mrs. Smith (neighbor)	555-5210

On the lines below, write your own telephone list. Use a telephone book to check the numbers. Include the names and numbers of at least five friends or relatives you know that you might call for help.

Place or Person	Telephone Number

End Punctuation

Surf's Up!

Surfing can be an <u>engaging</u> sport. Those who do it really enjoy it. In 1985, the first inland surfing <u>contest</u> was held in Allentown, Pennsylvania. What's unusual about that? There isn't an ocean within 200 miles of Allentown! Machines made the three-foot to five-foot waves that the <u>competitors</u> rode.

Some 300,000 people went to Big Surf at Tempe, Arizona in 1986. Even though the ocean is hundreds of miles away, they enjoyed Big Surf's machine-made waves. There they could body surf, ride a rented surf board, or slide down the 300-foot surf slide. When the surfers became <u>exhausted</u>, they could lie on the beach and enjoy the sand and the sun. If you didn't know better, you might think they were on a California beach, waiting for a wave.

Read the story carefully. Study the words before and after each underlined word. They will help you understand what the underlined word means.

Building Vocabulary Circle the letter of the word or words in the box below that mean almost the same as the underlined words.

1. <u>engaging</u>	a. expensive	b. pleasing	c. boring	d. difficult
2. <u>contest</u>	a. competition	b. party	c. school test	d. meeting
3. <u>competitors</u>	a. friends	b. strangers	c. those in a contest	d. contest judges
4. <u>exhausted</u>	a. silly	b. hardened	c. happy	d. tired

Check your choices in a dictionary. Add these words and their meanings to your vocabulary notebook. Try to use them as often as you can.

Each kind of sentence has its own end punctuation mark.

- A **declarative sentence** (a statement) ends with a period: **I think surfing is a terrific sport.**

- An **imperative sentence** (a command) also ends with a period: **Try it.**

- An **interrogative sentence** (a question) ends with a question mark: **Did you have fun surfing?**

- An **exclamatory sentence** (shows strong feeling) ends with an exclamation mark: **What fun surfing is!**

Try It

Add the correct end mark to each sentence. Check your answers on page 128.

1. Surfing is sometimes done far from an ocean_____

2. Have you ever gone surfing_____

3. What an exciting sport surfing is_____

4. Come surfing with me_____

This is a warm-up exercise. If you make two or more mistakes, read the definitions and examples on page 126 again before working exercise A.

A Identifying End Marks

In the space after each sentence, write C if the correct end mark is used. If the end mark is incorrect, write the correct mark in the space.

1. Is riding a surfboard easy. _____

2. Lie face down on the board and go out past the waves. _____

3. Swim with the board in front of a wave at least three feet high! _____

4. Can you stand up as the wave starts to lift the board. _____

5. What an exciting ride you will have? _____

6. Surfers shift their weight to steer a board. _____

7. They steer the board across the face of a wave? _____

If you need help, check the rules on page 126.

B Adding End Marks

Add the correct end mark to each of the following sentences.

1. Did you know there are 10 kinds of surfing_____

2. Most surfers do surfboard riding_____

3. That sport is most often called surfing_____

4. Did you know that body surfing is another way to surf_____

5. Let's look at body surfing first_____

6. Body surfing is done without a board_____

7. What fun it is to body surf_____

8. Swim out to meet the wave, then turn to face the shore_____

9. Dive towards the shore and let the wave carry you_____

Number Missed	0	1	2	3	4	5	6	7	8	9	10	11	12	13	14	15	16
Percent Correct	100	94	88	81	75	69	63	56	50	44	38	31	25	19	13	6	0

C Proofreading   There are six errors in the following paragraph. Put missing punctuation marks where they belong. Cross out each other error and write the correction above it. The first one has been done for you. You should find five more.

know

Those who ~~knows~~ how to surf can stand at the front of the board. Those

who are just learning should stand near the middle of the board. it is easier

to steer the board when you stand in the middle of it. Some surfers can do

tricks on a bord. They do 360s by turning the board in a circle. They do

roller coasters by riding up and down the face of a wave Don't get fancy on

a board until you can stear it well.

You should find and correct the following errors:
- 1 word that should be capitalized
- 1 missing punctuation mark
- 1 incorrect punctuation mark
- 2 misspelled words

D Writing Sentences   Answer each question in a complete sentence. If you need help, review the story on page 126 and exercises A and B.

1. Is there more than one way to surf? _____

_____

_____

2. Why does body surfing cost less than surfing? _____

_____

_____

3. Is it necessary to go to an ocean to surf? _____

_____

_____

4. Would you like to go surfing? Why or why not? _____

_____

_____

5. Where would you like to go surfing? Why? _____

_____

_____

Remember to begin each sentence with a capital letter. End each sentence with the correct punctuation mark.

Try It Answers for page 127

1. .
2. ?
3. !
4. .

Number Missed	0	1	2	3	4	5	6	7	8	9	10
Percent Correct	100	90	80	70	60	50	40	30	20	10	0

Focus on Writing

Completing an Entry Form

Have you ever entered a contest? Imagine that the Go-Now Travel Company is having a contest. The winner will receive a free trip to anywhere in the world. To enter, you must complete a form. If you do a good job of answering the questions, you could be the winner. Complete the contest entry form below.

GO-NOW TRAVEL COMPANY

Contest Entry Form

Contest rules: People of all ages may enter this contest. The winner will receive a trip to any place of her or his choice. The winner must (a) answer all questions clearly and (b) show an interest in travel. The decision of the judges will be final.

1. Name_____

   Address_____

   _____

2. Telephone Number_____

3. What place would you like to visit? Give reasons for your choice in no more than 30 words. Write complete sentences. _____

   _____

   _____

   _____

   _____

   _____

4. How is travel helpful to people? Explain your answer in no more than 30 words. _____

   _____

   _____

   _____

   _____

Commas

I WANT YOU
FOR U.S. ARMY
NEAREST RECRUITING STATION

Who Was Uncle Sam?

The name "Uncle Sam" stands for our country or government. Most people have seen a picture of Uncle Sam. He wears a tall hat with stars and stripes. He has long hair and a white beard. A World War I <u>poster</u> of a <u>scowling</u> Uncle Sam shows him pointing his finger. The words on the poster say, "I want you for the U. S. Army." Who was Uncle Sam?

One story says that Samuel Wilson was an army meat <u>inspector</u> during the War of 1812. He stamped the barrels of meat "U. S.," for United States. One man asked what the <u>initials</u> U. S. stood for. As a joke, someone said they stood for the meat inspector, Uncle Sam. The name stuck.

Read the story carefully. Study the words before and after each underlined word. They will help you understand what the underlined word means.

Building Vocabulary   Circle the letter of the word or words in the box below that mean almost the same as the underlined words.

1. <u>poster</u>	a. stamps	b. book	c. picture	d. TV show
2. <u>scowling</u>	a. laughing	b. fighting	c. speaking	d. frowning
3. <u>inspector</u>	a. one who looks at closely b. one who owns a store		c. one who cleans up d. one who raises animals	
4. <u>initials</u>	a. first names b. first letters of a name		c. last names d. all letters in a name	

Check your choices in a dictionary. Add these words and their meanings to your vocabulary notebook. Try to use them as often as possible.

Use **commas** for the following reasons.

To Separate Three or More Words or Word Groups in a Series

• We bought meat, milk, and bread.   • I will work, eat, and go home.

To Set Off Words That Interrupt or Give Extra Information

• Ida, who is my best friend, is coming.   • She's late, as usual.

To Set Off Words Such As <u>Yes</u>, <u>No</u>, **and** <u>Well</u>

• Well, we did it.   • Yes, I think you're right.

To Set Off Names of People Being Spoken To

• What's wrong, Tad?   • Mario, please pass the pepper.

The word <u>and</u> or <u>or</u> often comes before the last word in a series. Use a comma before <u>and</u> or <u>or</u> in a series.

You will learn about other uses of commas in the Handbook on page 156.

Try It
Add commas where they are needed in the following sentences. Check your answers on page 132.

1. No I did not know if Uncle Sam was a real person or not.

2. I have not read that story in newspapers magazines or books.

3. Some man just for a joke said that U. S. stood for Uncle Sam.

4. Jenny please read everything you can about Uncle Sam.

This is a warm-up exercise. If you make two or more mistakes, read the definitions and examples on page 130 again before working exercise A.

A Finding Places Where Commas Are Needed
Add commas wherever they are needed in the following sentences. Commas do not need to be added to all sentences.

1. Pictures of Uncle Sam which often appear in newspapers have changed.

2. Yes he was first shown as a young man without a beard.

3. The Uncle Sam shown sitting in a chair looked very tired.

4. Martha did you know that the name Uncle Sam was once an insult?

5. Well I suppose some countries did not like the United States.

6. In addition some people in this country used that term to show their anger with the government.

7. The name Uncle Sam which may have come from a meat inspector first appeared in 1813.

8. Then it was used in the book *The Adventures of Uncle Sam.*

9. Soon it would be used in letters posters and other reading matter.

10. Uncle Sam's suit with its stars and stripes was drawn in the 1830s.

If you need help, review the rules for the uses of commas on page 130.

early Uncle Sam

B Completing Sentences
Choose words from the box below to complete each sentence. Be sure to copy all commas and end marks that are shown.

| , in 1961, | ads, posters, and stamps. | , Vera? | , who was playing a joke, |

1. Where have you seen Uncle Sam's picture _____

2. I have seen Uncle Sam's picture on _____

3. One man _____ invented Uncle Sam.

4. Our Congress _____ made Uncle Sam the symbol of our country.

Complete the sentences you are sure of first. Mark off the word groups as you use them. Then go back to the sentences that you left blank. Find the correct word groups left on the list.

Number Missed	0	1	2	3	4	5	6	7	8	9	10	11	12	13	14	15	16
Percent Correct	100	94	88	81	75	69	63	56	50	44	38	31	25	19	13	6	0

C Using Commas   Use your own words to complete each sentence. Your words should either add a series to the sentence or add extra information. For information to complete each sentence, look again at the opening story and at exercise A. Don't forget to use commas where they are needed.

1. Samuel Wilson _____

_____ was an army meat inspector during the War of 1812.

2. _____ did you know that the U.S. he stamped on the barrels of meat stood for United States?

3. Someone _____

_____ asked what the initials U.S. stood for.

4. It was not long before Uncle Sam's picture began appearing in _____

_____ .

Use words that give extra information in sentences 1, 2, and 3. Use words in a series in sentence 4.

D Proofreading   There are six errors in the following paragraph. Put punctuation marks where they belong. Cross out other errors and write corrections above them. The first error is marked for you. You should find five more.

               Uncle
The first pictures of ~~uncle~~ Sam show him wearing a robe. The robe was

covered with stars and stripes. Dan Rice a clown during the 1800s wore a

costume like that. People began to accept it as Uncle Sams clothing. It was

not until President Lincolns time that Uncle Sam was given a beard and his

famous tall hat

You should find and correct these errors:
- *1 missing end mark*
- *2 missing commas*
- *2 missing apostrophes*

E Writing Sentences   Answer each question with a complete sentence. Be sure to use commas where they are needed.

1. Was Uncle Sam, the symbol of our country, a real person? _____

_____

2. Do you think England, France, and other countries have symbols? _____

_____

3. Did Dan Rice draw a picture of Uncle Sam for the newspaper? _____

_____

Try It Answers for page 131

1. No,
2. newspapers, magazines,
3. man, just for a joke,
4. Jenny,

Number Missed	0	1	2	3	4	5	6	7	8	9	10	11	12
Percent Correct	100	92	83	75	67	58	50	42	33	25	17	8	0

Focus on Writing

Writing a
Descriptive
Paragraph

Uncle Sam is a symbol of our country. Does your community have a symbol? Imagine that you have been asked to design one. The symbol may be a man, woman, teenager, or child. Use a real person as a model if you wish. Think about these questions.

- What does the person look like?
- How is he or she dressed?
- What is the person doing?
- Is he or she holding anything?
- How does the person stand for the spirit and customs in your community?

On the lines below, write a paragraph telling how your symbol will look. Be sure to include details about color, shape, and size. For example, if the person is wearing a hat, tell exactly what the hat looks like. Also tell why certain details are used. Is the person holding something, such as a flower? If so, explain how it stands for your community.

_____

_____

_____

_____

_____

_____

_____

In the space below, draw a picture of your symbol.

Quotation Marks

Rocking to the Top

Elvis Presley (1935–1977) was one of the first important rock stars. He was the first to <u>impress</u> huge audiences with this new music, which used a strong <u>rhythm</u>, the electric guitar, and other sounds.

Many adults were shocked by Presley's performances. They felt that he was not a <u>suitable</u> model for young people. Some high schools would not allow students to dress like Presley. Rock 'n Roll was said to be dangerous. However, young people <u>responded</u> well to Presley's music. He made dozens of best-selling records and starred in 33 films during a career that lasted more than 20 years.

> Read the story carefully. Study the words before and after each underlined word. They will help you understand what the underlined word means.

Building Vocabulary   Circle the letter of the word or words in the box below that mean almost the same as the underlined words.

1. <u>impress</u>	a. disturb	b. give	c. please	d. begin
2. <u>rhythm</u>	a. repeated beat	b. sad songs	c. country western	d. loud music
3. <u>suitable</u>	a. bad	b. possible	c. proper	d. incorrect
4. <u>responded</u>	a. joined	b. reacted	c. danced	d. showed

> Check your choices in a dictionary. Add these words and their meanings to your vocabulary notebook. Try to use them as often as possible.

Use **quotation marks** before and after a quote, or a speaker's exact words. Words called **speaker words** often come before, after, or in the middle of a quote. The speaker words below are underlined. Notice how commas are used to set off the speaker words from the quote. When the speaker words come before the quote, the comma is outside the quotation marks. If the speaker words come after the quote, the comma is inside the quotation marks. If the speaker words come in the middle, the first comma is inside the quotation marks and the second comma is outside.

- <u>Lana said</u>, "I think that his music is great." (comma is outside quote)

- "I think that his music is great," <u>Lana said</u>. (comma is inside quote)

- "I think," <u>Lana said</u>, "that his music is great." (first comma is inside quote; second comma is outside quote)

> When the exact words end a sentence, the end punctuation mark is always inside the quotation marks.
>
> Quotation marks are also used around the titles of magazine articles, short stories, poems, and songs. See page 156 of the Handbook.

Try It

Add quotation marks and commas where they are needed in the following sentences. Check your answers on page 136.

1. Do you like Elvis Presley's records? Janet asked me.

2. Yes I answered I do.

3. Roberto said My father has a good collection of his records.

4. I'm writing a report on Elvis Presley said John.

5. Why Beth asked do you think Elvis was so popular?

This is a warm-up exercise. If you make two or more mistakes, read the definitions and examples on page 134 again before working exercise A.

A Using Quotation Marks and Commas

Add quotation marks and commas where they are needed in the following sentences. Remember to use commas correctly to set off speaker words from a quote.

1. What Presley records do you like best? I asked my friend.

2. I like every record he ever made answered Ted.

3. My cousin said He made many songs very popular.

4. I liked to watch him sing in his movies my mother told me.

5. Presley's songs had a strong beat said my father.

6. Many people my father added really admired his voice.

7. Yes my mother agreed all my friends thought it was fantastic.

8. A number of his songs were about love my friend pointed out.

9. My aunt said Many of his songs were quite sad.

10. Wasn't he a powerful performer? asked my mother.

11. In my opinion Marco said he was the best.

12. Cheryl explained He sang many of his best songs in his movies.

13. Listen to this great song Sabra said as she put on a record.

14. Have you ever seen Elvis Presley on a video? Abbie asked me.

15. I think I saw one of his videos answered my father.

16. I remember the time I went to one of his concerts said my mother.

17. We sat all the way in the back of the theater she said.

When the exact words end with a question mark, no comma is used to separate the exact words from the speaker words.

Number Missed	0	1	2	3	4	5	6	7	8	9	10	11	12	13	14	15	16	17	18	19	20	21	22	23	24	25	26	27	28	29	30	31	32	33	34
Percent Correct	100	98	96	95	93	91	89	88	86	84	82	81	79	77	75	74	72	70	68	67	65	63	61	60	58	56	54	53	51	49	47	46	44	42	40

Number Missed	35	36	37	38	39	40	41	42	43	44	45	46	47	48	49	50	51	52	53	54	55	56	57
Percent Correct	39	37	35	33	32	30	28	26	25	23	21	19	18	16	14	12	11	9	7	5	4	2	0

Lesson 29 Part 3 Quotation Marks ■■■■■■■■■■■■■■■■■■

B Using Quotation Marks

Use your own words to complete the following sentences. Remember to add commas and quotation marks wherever they belong.

1. I think that Elvis Presley, Wendy said _____
   _____

2. After listening to some Presley records, Mother said _____
   _____

3. I'm not sure said Sara _____
   _____

4. _____
   _____ said my older brother.

If you need help, review the rules on page 134.

C Proofreading

There are six errors in the following paragraph. Put punctuation marks where they belong. Cross out each other error and write the correction above it. The first one has been done for you. You should find five more.

                             helped

For many years, Colonel Tom Parker ~~help~~ Elvis Presley. He got Presley a contract with RCA in 1955. He help him become popular Presley made his first film in 1956. after serving in the Army, he stops singing in public. Then Parker brought him back with a big TV show in 1968 The singer seemed to be as popular as ever.

You should find and correct the following errors:
- *1 word that should be capitalized*
- *2 incorrect verb forms*
- *2 missing punctuation marks*

D Writing Sentences

Write three sentences of your own about Elvis Presley or another popular singer. Include quotes and speaker words in each sentence. Use quotation marks, commas, and end punctuation correctly.

1. _____
   _____

2. _____
   _____

3. _____
   _____

Try It Answers for page 135

1. "Do . . . records?" Janet asked me.
2. "Yes," I answered, "I do."
3. Roberto said, "My . . . records."
4. "I'm . . . Presley," said John.
5. "Why," Beth asked, "do . . . popular?"

Number Missed	0	1	2	3	4	5	6	7	8	9	10	11	12
Percent Correct	100	92	83	75	67	58	50	42	33	25	17	8	0

Focus on Writing

Writing
Answers to
Questions

Many articles are written about famous people like Elvis Presley. Suppose that an article will be written about <u>you</u>. A reporter from the school paper will ask you questions. Below are the questions the reporter will ask. Write your answer to each one.

Reporter: Tell me about yourself. What things do you enjoy most?

You: _____

_____

_____

Write your answers in complete sentences. Quotation marks are not needed in this style of writing.

Reporter: What new things would you like to try? Are there some things you haven't had time for yet but would like to do?

You: _____

_____

_____

_____

Reporter: What about the people in your life? Who are some of the people most important to you?

You: _____

_____

_____

Reporter: What is one thing you are very proud of?

You: _____

_____

_____

Reporter: What do you plan to do when you finish school?

You: _____

_____

_____

Apostrophes

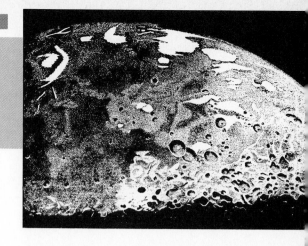

One Small Step

For years, people <u>conjectured</u> about the moon. What was it made of? What was it like? Could people <u>exist</u> on it? Those questions were answered on July 20, 1969. On that day, two men stepped onto the moon for the first time.

As Neil Armstrong left the lunar lander, he let down a TV camera. Over 500 million people <u>observed</u> him as he stepped onto the moon. "That's one small step for [a] man, one giant step for mankind," he told them.

Armstrong and Edwin Aldrin <u>accumulated</u> rocks to show scientists back on the earth what the moon was made of. They planted an American flag. They left a metal marker where they landed. The marker said, "Here men from the planet earth first set foot upon the moon July, 1969 A.D. We came in peace for all mankind."

> Read the story carefully. Study the words before and after each underlined word. They will help you understand what the underlined word means.

Building Vocabulary Circle the letter of the word or words in the box below that mean almost the same as the underlined words.

1. <u>conjecture</u>	a. wonder	b. circle	c. hear	d. travel
2. <u>exist</u>	a. recall	b. walk	c. destroy	d. live
3. <u>observe</u>	a. cheer	b. copy	c. watch	d. wait
4. <u>accumulate</u>	a. praise	b. gather	c. change	d. place

> Check your choices in a dictionary. Add these words and their meanings to your vocabulary notebook. Try to use them as often as possible.

Use an **apostrophe** to show ownership, or possession.

- the boy's coat (the coat of the boy)

- the boys' coats (the coats of more than one boy)

- children's names (names of more than one child)

An apostrophe in a **contraction** shows that one or more letters are missing.

- they're = they are
- can't = can not
- doesn't = does not

- isn't = is not
- he'll = he will
- I've = I have

- hasn't = has not
- she's = she is
- it's = it is

For a review of the possessive, see page 10.

For a complete list of common contractions, see page 155 of the Handbook.

Try It

Cross out each word that needs an apostrophe in the following sentences. Write the word correctly above it. Check your answers on page 140.

1. There were few people who didnt see the *Eagle* land on the moon.

2. The ships passengers were eager to land.

3. Neil Armstrongs boot was filmed as he stepped onto the moon.

4. They found it wasnt too hard to move around on the moon.

5. The flag they put there wont wave, because there is no wind.

This is a warm-up exercise. If you make two or more mistakes, read the definitions and examples again on page 138 before working exercise A.

A Using Apostrophes Correctly

Cross out each word that needs an apostrophe in the following sentences. Write the word correctly above it.

If you need help, review the definitions and examples on page 138. For a complete list of common contractions, see page 155 of the Handbook.

1. One man on that space flight cant step onto the moon.

2. Michael Collins circles the moons surface in the *Columbia*.

3. TV news people tell us whos flying the *Columbia*.

4. The first mans feet are on the surface of the moon.

5. He says its covered with powder.

6. Im sure I saw the second astronaut leave the *Eagle*.

7. Now theyre both hopping about on the moon.

8. Doesnt it look as though they are having fun?

9. Lets watch Armstrong and Aldrin set up the American flag.

10. I hope you dont think that the first walk on the moon was easy.

11. It was our countrys dream for many years.

12. The space programs cameras had filmed the moon.

13. There were few landing places the men hadnt studied on film.

14. We werent leaving too much to chance.

15. In one persons words, the moon rocks were worth more than gold.

16. Whats the reason for leaving cameras on the moon?

Number Missed	0	1	2	3	4	5	6	7	8	9	10	11	12	13	14	15	16
Percent Correct	100	94	88	81	75	69	63	56	50	44	38	31	25	19	13	6	0

Lesson 30 Part 3 Apostrophes ■■■■■■■■■■■■■■■■■■■■

B Writing Words with Apostrophes Write each sentence. Change the underlined words to a possessive or a contraction. Be sure to use the apostrophe correctly.

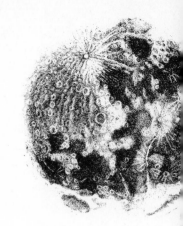

1. I did not see the moon landing.

_____

2. A friend of my father saw it on his TV set.

_____

3. He thinks the space program is not exciting now.

_____

C Proofreading There are six errors in the following paragraph. Put missing punctuation marks where they belong. Cross out each error and write the correction above it. The first one has been done for you. You should find five more.

               gives
    The moon give off no light of its own. The moons light is really the sun's light. The moon reflects, or casts back, the light it recieves from the sun. Lets just say that it shines. On some nights, the moon appear to be a big, round ball. On other nights, it appears to be a thin slice of light The moon does not change its size or shape. Different parts are lighted by the sun at different times.

You should find and correct the following errors:
- 1 incorrect verb form
- 1 missing punctuation mark
- 1 misspelled word
- 2 words that need an apostrophe

D Writing Sentences Turn each sentence into a question. Use the contraction or the possessive correctly when you write the question. Begin each question with the word that is underlined in each statement.

1. You dont follow the work of NASA. _____

_____

2. NASAs job is to run the space program. _____

_____

3. You didnt know about the space station. _____

_____

Try It Answers for page 139

1. didn't
2. ship's
3. Armstrong's
4. wasn't
5. won't

Number Missed	0	1	2	3	4	5	6	7	8	9	10	11
Percent Correct	100	91	82	73	64	55	45	36	27	18	9	0

Focus on Writing

Writing a Schedule

Imagine that a famous person, such as an astronaut, will spend a day in your school. You are in charge of planning the events for this special day. The visitor will arrive at 9:00 A.M. sharp. You decide to first take the guest on a short tour of your school. You might include the library, two or three classrooms, and any places of special interest. Then the visitor will give a talk to all the students. Following this, there will be a time for students to ask the visitor questions. Lunch comes next. During the afternoon, there will be one or more activities by students. There might, for example, be a skit or a play. There could be a musical program or activities in the gym. Choose something you think the visitor would enjoy.

Give the time each event should begin and end, for example 9:00 A.M. to 9:45 A.M.

On the lines below, write a schedule for the day. Keep in mind that the visitor must catch a plane at 4:00 P.M. The ride to the airport takes 35 minutes. Think carefully about how long each event will take.

Event	Time	Place

A **Using Capital Letters**   Circle each word that should begin with a capital letter. For help, review page 122.

1. Martha said, "the play was interesting."

2. One of my favorite writers was E. B. white.

3. please don't be late for dinner, today.

4. It was not i who asked about camping.

5. Sometimes, I help mr. Watson mow his lawn.

6. I read a short story called "Four Strikes and you're Really Out."

7. I called dr. Wong when I cut my hand.

8. "Egypt," Sarah said, "is an african country."

9. Wayne said, "tomorrow's weather should be good."

10. Did you ever read the book *The wizard of Oz?*

11. are you going to Toni's party?

12. I must finish this paper for miss Salvo's English class.

13. My dog, bambi, is a loveable animal.

14. "On the other hand," marlene said, "it is early."

15. "I don't know where to put the mexican rug," Mrs. Cole told her friend.

B **Using End Punctuation**   End each sentence with the correct mark. For help, review page 126.

1. Who has change for a quarter____

2. I can give you a dime and three nickels____

3. Tell those children not to play in the street____

4. What a beautiful sight that was____

5. Come to the library with me this afternoon____

6. Shall we walk, or ride our bicycles____

7. Some day, next week, I am going on a picnic with my friends____

8. What a wonderful idea____

9. How bright the moon is tonight____

10. Please make your bed before you come down to breakfast____

Number Missed	0	1	2	3	4	5	6	7	8	9	10	11	12	13	14	15	16	17	18	19	20	21	22	23	24	25
Percent Correct	100	96	92	88	84	80	76	72	68	64	60	56	52	48	44	40	36	32	28	24	20	16	12	8	4	0

142

C Using Commas   Add commas where they are needed in the following sentences. For help, review page 130.

1. The bus for example was ten minutes early this morning.

2. Yes I saw Agnes and Marcia at the show.

3. That movie which is the funniest I've seen is still playing.

4. Alan did you take a message for me?

5. I have paper pencils and pens on my desk.

6. Let us know when you are ready Pam.

7. I go to that class on Monday Wednesday and Friday.

8. My cousins flying a kite had a wonderful time at the beach.

9. We raked grass leaves and sticks from the front lawn.

10. Well I think you are teasing me.

D Using Quotation Marks   Add quotation marks and commas where they are needed in the following sentences. For help, review page 134.

1. Fran asked Did you read the article in today's paper?

2. The weather reporter said There is a good chance of rain.

3. What Walter asked is the use?

4. The roast said Allyson is in the oven.

5. Where is the light switch? asked Marvin.

E Using Apostrophes   Add apostrophes where they are needed in the following sentences. For help, review page 138.

1. He said theyre coming later.

2. The store had a sale on boys shoes.

3. Do your mother and Aunt Mae belong to the same womens club?

4. I can sing, but I cant play the piano.

5. You wont have to feed the dog again until after dinner.

6. He stepped in the garden and broke one plants stem.

7. We have to trim both cats claws.

8. After Ive asked a question, tell me the answer.

Number Missed	0	1	2	3	4	5	6	7	8	9	10	11	12	13	14	15	16	17	18	19	20	21	22	23	24
Percent Correct	100	98	95	93	91	89	86	84	82	80	77	75	73	70	68	66	64	61	59	57	55	52	50	48	45

Number Missed	25	26	27	28	29	30	31	32	33	34	35	36	37	38	39	40	41	42	43	44
Percent Correct	43	41	39	36	34	32	30	27	25	23	20	18	16	14	11	9	7	5	2	0

Practice Test: Lessons 26–30 Part I ■■■■■■■■■■■■■■■

A Capital Letters Read the sentences. Some words are capitalized which should not be. Others need to be capitalized. Find the letter of the word that is wrong. Blacken the circle for that choice in the answer box to the right.

1. I have just finished reading the book *great Expectations*.
   a. I   b. reading   c. book   d. great

2. everyone, including Randy, will hide while Peggy counts to 100.
   a. everyone   b. Randy   c. will   d. Peggy

3. We invited col. and Mrs. Edward A. Young to the party.
   a. We   b. col.   c. Mrs.   d. A.

4. This is the Street where my family and I live.
   a. This   b. Street   c. family   d. I

5. Mother, may my Friend Sandra Loo come for lunch?
   a. Mother   b. Friend   c. Sandra   d. lunch

6. How many times must i ask you to close the door?
   a. How   b. i   c. you   d. door

7. Mexico, the United States, and Canada are North american countries.
   a. United States   b. Canada   c. North american   d. countries

8. Did you ever read the poem "Song for a Rainy day"?
   a. Did   b. poem   c. Rainy   d. day

9. Which is the longest River in the United States?
   a. Which   b. longest   c. River   d. the

1. (a) (b) (c) (d)
2. (a) (b) (c) (d)
3. (a) (b) (c) (d)
4. (a) (b) (c) (d)
5. (a) (b) (c) (d)
6. (a) (b) (c) (d)
7. (a) (b) (c) (d)
8. (a) (b) (c) (d)
9. (a) (b) (c) (d)

B End Punctuation Read the three sentences in each group. Find the letter of the sentence that ends correctly. Blacken the circle of that letter in the answer box to the right.

10. a. Give me your hand.
    b. Give me your hand?
    c. Give me your hand!

11. a. My family built this house?
    b. My family built this house!
    c. My family built this house.

12. a. How did you learn to swim that well?
    b. How did you learn to swim that well!
    c. How did you learn to swim that well.

10. (a) (b) (c)
11. (a) (b) (c)
12. (a) (b) (c)

Number Missed	0	1	2	3	4	5	6	7	8	9	10	11	12
Percent Correct	100	92	83	75	67	58	50	42	33	25	17	8	0

144

C Commas

Some commas have been left out of the following sentences. Find the letter of the word that should be <u>followed</u> by a comma. Blacken the circle for that choice in the answer box to the right.

Answer Box

1. Most of the socks that I own are black blue, or gray.
   a. socks   b. own   c. are   d. black

   1. ⓐ ⓑ ⓒ ⓓ

2. Will you do an errand for me after school this afternoon Leo?
   a. errand   b. me   c. school   d. afternoon

   2. ⓐ ⓑ ⓒ ⓓ

3. No I don't think you left your book on the bus.
   a. No   b. don't   c. think   d. book

   3. ⓐ ⓑ ⓒ ⓓ

4. Yesterday I helped my father wash and wax the family car which is new.
   a. Yesterday   b. father   c. wash   d. car

   4. ⓐ ⓑ ⓒ ⓓ

5. In addition you will have to put aside some money for your trip.
   a. addition   b. have   c. aside   d. money

   5. ⓐ ⓑ ⓒ ⓓ

D Quotation Marks

Some quotation marks have been left out of the following sentences. Find the letter of the word that should have quotation marks <u>in front of it</u>. Blacken the circle for that choice in the answer box to the right.

6. I think that is a nice song," said Bill.
   a. I   b. that   c. said   d. song

   6. ⓐ ⓑ ⓒ ⓓ

7. "I did not," Michael said, ask him to come."
   a. did   b. said   c. ask   d. to

   7. ⓐ ⓑ ⓒ ⓓ

8. Wendy asked, Who wrote the book *The Courage of Sarah Noble?*"
   a. asked   b. Who   c. book   d. The

   8. ⓐ ⓑ ⓒ ⓓ

9. Did you read that long chapter last night?" asked Andrew.
   a. Did   b. read   c. last   d. Andrew

   9. ⓐ ⓑ ⓒ ⓓ

E Apostrophes

Find the letter of the word that needs an apostrophe. Blacken the circle for that choice in the answer box to the right.

10. I must remember to repair the dogs collar when I get a chance.
    a. remember   b. repair   c. dogs   d. chance

    10. ⓐ ⓑ ⓒ ⓓ

11. You are going to the show with me tomorrow, arent you?
    a. You   b. are   c. tomorrow   d. arent

    11. ⓐ ⓑ ⓒ ⓓ

12. Julie said shell buy the lunch if we buy the tickets.
    a. shell   b. lunch   c. we   d. tickets

    12. ⓐ ⓑ ⓒ ⓓ

Number Missed	0	1	2	3	4	5	6	7	8	9	10	11	12
Percent Correct	100	92	83	75	67	58	50	42	33	25	17	8	0

Handbook

1 Glossary of Grammar Terms and Definitions

The number in parentheses refers to the lesson in which the term is first defined.

adjective (12) A word that describes, or tells something about, a noun.

yellow daisy   small building
comfortable chair

adjective clause (23) A group of words that has a subject and a predicate and is used as an adjective.

The joke **that David told** was very funny.

adverb (13) A word that describes, or tells something about, a verb, an adjective, or another adverb.

talked **quietly**   **very** happy   **always** late

adverb clause (22) A group of words that has a subject and a predicate and is used as an adverb.

When the clock struck midnight, we all went to bed.

agree (17) The subject and verb in a sentence must agree in number. If the subject is singular, the verb must be singular. If the subject is plural, the verb must be plural.

Singular: **She enjoys** football.
Plural: **They enjoy** soccer.

clause (22) A group of words that has a subject and a predicate and is used as part of a sentence. Some clauses can stand alone.

The bus was two hours late, and **we were all tired.**

Some clauses cannot stand alone.

Before the sun goes down.

common noun (1) The name of any person, place, or thing. A common noun begins with a small letter unless it starts a sentence.

woman   room   truck

complete predicate (15) All the words in a sentence that tell what a person or thing does or is.

The children **played in the pool all afternoon.**

complete subject (15) All the words that tell who or what the sentence is about.

The leaves on the tree are turning red.

compound predicate (18) A predicate made up of two or more verbs.

The car **sputtered** and **stopped.**

compound sentence (20) A group of words in which two sentences are joined by <u>and</u>, <u>or</u>, or <u>but</u>.

Suddenly, the lights went out, and then we heard a noise.

compound subject (18) A subject made up of two or more nouns or pronouns.

Maria and **Pete** write long letters to each other.

contraction (30) A short word that is formed by joining two other words.

can't   they've   I'm

declarative sentence (21) A sentence that makes a statement.

Gulls flew over the sandy white beach.

exclamatory sentence (21) A sentence that states a strong feeling.

I see a whale!

future tense (7) A verb form that tells about action in the future.

will call   will watch   will paint

helping verb (8) A verb that helps the main verb express action or make a statement.

are playing   **were** planning   **have** arrived

imperative sentence (21)   A sentence that gives a command.

> Stop throwing paper on the streets.

interrogative sentence (21)   A sentence that asks a question.

> Where is the toothpaste?

irregular verb (9)   A verb that does not form the past tense and past participle by adding -d or -ed.

> do/did/done   go/went/gone   see/saw/seen

main verb (8)   The second verb in two-word verbs.

> are **yelling**   has **stopped**   had **seen**

noun (1)   The name of a person, place, or thing.

> teacher   airport   telephone

object of a preposition (14)   A noun or pronoun that ends a prepositional phrase.

> from **Sally**   with the **family**   beside **him**

object pronoun (11)   A pronoun that is the object of a verb or a preposition.

> The ball hit **her**.   Jim walked home with **me**.

past participle (8)   A verb form that tells about action that happened in the past. It is used with a helping verb such as has or have.

> has **eaten**   have **taken**   had **finished**

past tense (6)   A verb form that tells about action that happened in the past.

> cooked   mowed   began

plural noun (2)   A noun that names more than one person, place, or thing.

> doctors   cities   dishes

possessive noun (3)   A noun that shows ownership.

> the cat's paws   the students' desks
> the women's jackets

possessive pronoun (5)   A pronoun that shows ownership.

> This is **my** toolbox.   That hammer is **yours**.

predicate (15)   The part of a sentence that tells what a person or thing does or is.

> The movie **is starting**.

preposition (14)   A word that shows how a noun or pronoun is connected to another word in a sentence.

> at   in   over   to   with

> Betsy likes working **in** the library.

prepositional phrase (14)   A group of words that starts with a preposition and ends with a noun or pronoun.

> into the water   above the door
> after the game

present participle (8)   A verb form that tells about action happening in the present. It is used with the helping verb am, are, is, was, or were.

> am **studying**   is **hoping**   were **talking**

present tense (6)   A verb form that tells about action happening in the present.

> works   laughs   ride

pronoun (4)   A word that takes the place of a noun.

> I   she   it   him   them

proper noun (1)   The name of a special person, place, or thing. A proper noun begins with one or more capital letters.

> Martin Luther King   Texas   July

regular verb (6)   A verb that forms the past tense and past participle by adding -d or -ed.

> walked   shoved   carried

relative pronoun (23)   The pronoun that, which, or who that links an adjective clause to a noun or pronoun in the main part of a sentence.

> The clock **that** I bought is broken.

> The days, **which** seemed like hours, sped by.

> He **who** hesitates is lost.

sentence (15)   A group of words about one idea. It must have a subject and a verb.

> **The tall ships sailed into the harbor.**

sentence fragment (19)   A group of words that does not express a complete idea.

> **After we finished.**

simple predicate (16)   The verb in the complete predicate in a sentence.

> Juan **jumped** over the fence.

simple subject (16)   The one person or thing a sentence is about.

> The **flowers** on the table are beautiful.

singular noun (2)   A noun that names one person, place, or thing.

> child   store   shirt

speaker words (29) The words that are used with a quotation and tell who is being quoted.

Marty said, "I'll meet you at the theater."

subject (15) The part of a sentence that tells the person or thing the sentence is about.

Aunt Marjorie will arrive tomorrow.

subject pronoun (5) A pronoun that can be the subject of a sentence.

I   you   he   she   it   we   they

verb (6) A word that usually shows action.

sings   howled   **threw**

verb be (10) A verb that has all irregular forms.

am   is   are   was   were

2 Spelling Rules

The rules below can help you spell many English words. There are a few exceptions when a rule does not apply. In most cases, however, these rules can guide you in your writing.

- Write i before e except after c, or when there is a long a sound.

  bel**ie**ve   fr**ie**nd   qu**ie**t   th**ie**f
  rec**ei**ve   c**ei**ling   dec**ei**ve
  eight   n**ei**ghbor   w**ei**gh   r**ei**ndeer

- Drop the final e when adding an ending that begins with a vowel.

  care + ing = car**ing**   date + ing = dat**ing**
  make + ing = mak**ing**

- Keep the final e when adding an ending that begins with a consonant.

  care + less = car**eless**   hope + ful = hop**eful**
  safe + ty = saf**ety**

- When a one-syllable word ends in one vowel followed by one consonant, double the consonant when adding an ending that begins with a vowel.

  swim, swim**ming**   plan, plan**ned**
  sad, sad**dest**

- When a word ends in a consonant followed by a y, change the y to i when adding an ending not beginning with i.

  cry, cr**ied**   silly, sill**iness**   funny, funn**ier**

- When a word ends in a vowel followed by a y, the word is not changed when an ending is added.

  enjoy, enjoy**ed**   play, play**ing**   pay, pay**ment**

3 Commonly Misspelled Words

This list contains words that people often spell incorrectly. Check this list when you proofread what you have written.

A		appearance	B	bulletin	certain
absence	against	applies	balance	buses	challenge
accidentally	agree	appreciate	bargain	business	changeable
accommodate	aisle	approach	basically	busy	character
accompanied	allowed	arctic	beauty		chief
accurately	all right	area	becoming	C	choose
accuses	already	argue	before	calendar	clothes
ache	always	arguing	beginning	campaign	color
achieve	among	athlete	belief	career	column
acquaintance	amount	athletic	believe	careless	comfortable
across	analyze	attempt	biscuit	carrying	coming
address	annual	attend	bracelet	catalogue	committed
admit	answer	attendance	breath	ceiling	companies
afraid	any	audience	breathe	cellar	competition
again	apologize	awfully	built	cemetery	completely

confident
conscience
conscious
considerably
continually
controlling
convenient
cooly
could
criticize
cruelty

D
decide
decision
definite
describe
desirable
develop
different
difficult
dining
disappear
disappoint
disease
division
doesn't
doubt
due
during
dying

E
easy
eighth
embarrass
emphasize
enough
entertainment
entrance
equipped
especially
every
excellent

exercise
exhaust
expensive
experience
extremely

F
familiar
families
fascinate
February
feminine
finally
foreign
forty
friend
fulfill
further

G
gauge
generally
government
guaranteed
guard
guess

H
half
happily
happiness
heavily
height
hopeful
hospital
huge
hundred

I
ideally
imaginary
imagine
immediately

incidentally
indefinite
instead
intelligence
interest
interrupt
island
itself

J
jealous
judgment
just

K
knowledge

L
language
leisure
library
license
lightning
loneliness
losing

M
manufacture
marriage
maybe
meadow
meant
mileage
minute
misspelled
muscle

N
necessary
neither
ninety
none
noticeable
nuisance

O
obedient
occasion
occasionally
occurred
often
omit
once
operate
opinion
opportunity
opposite
original
ought

P
paid
pastime
perform
performance
permanent
permission
personal
persuade
physical
physician
picnic
piece
pleasant
possess
possible
probably
procedure
proceed
prove
pursue

Q
quality
quantity
quart
quietly
quite

R
rabbit
raise
ready
really
receipt
receive
recommend
referred
regard
relief
relieve
religion
responsibility
restaurant
rhythm
ridiculous

S
safety
sandwich
satisfactory
schedule
scissors
seem
sense
separate
shining
significant
similar
sincerely
source
speech
straight
strength
stretch
stubborn
succeed
successful
surprise
surroundings

T
temperature

therefore
through
together
tomorrow
traffic
tries
trouble
truly
Tuesday
twelfth

U
unnecessary
useful
using

V
vacuum
various
vehicle
vinegar

W
weather
Wednesday
weight
weird
welcome
whether
whisper
whistle

Y
yawn
yield

4 Homophones

A number of words in English are confusing because they sound the same or almost the same but are spelled differently. Although they sound alike, the words have different meanings and different spellings. Here is a list of some common homophones.

aloud out loud
The teacher read the story **aloud**.

allowed permitted
No pets were **allowed** in the hotel.

all ready all are ready
Let me know when you are **all ready** to begin.

already before
I **already** bought my ticket.

all together everyone at the same time
We will sing the song **all together**.

altogether completely
The sand washed away **altogether**.

assistance help; aid
The injured received **assistance** right away.

assistants helpers
The head coach had three **assistants**.

attendance being present
My brother's **attendance** at school is perfect.

attendants persons who wait on others
Three **attendants** helped the visitors.

beat to strike or hit
My sister **beat** the drum.

beet a red vegetable
The chef sliced a cooked **beet**.

blew the past tense of the verb *blow*
A strong wind **blew** all night long.

blue the color of the sky on a clear day
The man wore a dark **blue** suit.

brake a device for stopping
He put on the emergency **brake** before leaving the car.

break to separate into parts; shatter
We tried to **break** the sheet of plastic into two pieces.

capital the place where a government is located
Montpelier is the **capital** of Vermont.

capitol the building in which a legislature meets
The **capitol** building was finished in 1811.

cent a penny
I don't have a **cent** left.

scent a pleasant odor
Is that the **scent** of roses?

sent the past tense of *send*
He **sent** the letter.

cereal a food prepared from grain
I eat **cereal** for breakfast every morning.

serial something produced in installments
That television **serial** lasted three years.

cite to quote as an example
The lawyer **cited** three state laws.

sight the ability to see
A person's **sight** is very valuable.

site the place that an event happens
The Pilgrims landed at this **site**.

close to shut
Please **close** the door.

clothes items that one wears
Sally bought new **clothes** for the party.

coarse rough; uneven
The walkway was covered with **coarse** stones.

course a path over which something moves
An earthquake changed the **course** of the river.

fair pleasant
The weather will be **fair** for the next three days.

fair just
The judge's decision was most **fair**.

fare payment for passage
The bus **fare** to the city is $1.50.

its a possessive pronoun
The horse took **its** place in the starting gate.

it's the contraction for *it is*
It's going to be nice tomorrow.

for	a preposition This letter is **for** Andrew.
fore	toward the front The **fore** part of the ship was damaged.
four	one more than three I have **four** clean shirts.
forth	into view The crowd came **forth** from the stadium.
fourth	after the third The team was in **fourth** place.
heal	to make well Your finger will **heal** in a day or two.
heel	the built-up portion of a shoe One **heel** is higher than the other.
he'll	the contraction for *he will* **He'll** help us on Saturday.
hear	to receive sound by means of the ear I can **hear** the speaker very well.
here	at or in this place Put the package **here**.
knew	the past tense of *know* I **knew** of a shortcut through the woods.
new	recently made The **new** penny was very shiny.
lead	a heavy metal The suitcase was as heavy as **lead**.
led	the past tense of *lead* I **led** the group along the narrow path.
loan	something borrowed I will ask the bank for a **loan**.
lone	all alone A **lone** tree grew in the open field.
made	the past tense of *make* I **made** lunch this afternoon.
maid	a female servant The **maid** cleaned the room.
mail	letters and packages in a postal system Has the **mail** come yet?
male	of the male sex Roscoe is our **male** cat.

passed	the past tense of *pass* A car **passed** us on the narrow road.
past	time gone by Everyone should know something about the **past**.
peace	a state of calm or quiet **Peace** is always better than war.
piece	a part of something We each received a **piece** of cake.
pole	a long, rounded piece of wood The telephone **pole** held ten wires.
poll	a survey The **poll** reported how people felt.
principal	the head of a school The **principal** spoke at the assembly.
principle	a basic truth That is the **principle** we believe in.
road	an open way for passage This **road** has a lot of curves.
rode	the past tense of *ride* We **rode** on the bus for three hours.
rowed	the past tense of *row* We **rowed** the boat across the river.
role	a function or job What **role** did you play in the decision?
roll	to travel on wheels The car will **roll** off the road.
sail	to manage a ship or boat The ferry will **sail** shortly before noon.
sale	to exchange for money I will arrange for the **sale** of the house.
their	a possessive pronoun They all took **their** places.
there	a place We will be **there** in five minutes.
they're	the contraction for *they are* **They're** tired from the long walk.
threw	the past tense of *throw* The pitcher **threw** perfectly.
through	in one side and out the other A train passed **through** the tunnel ten minutes ago.

to	a preposition or word that marks a verb Did they give the answer **to** you? It's dangerous **to** stay here.	**waist**	the part of the body between the ribs and pelvis She wore a thin belt around her **waist**.
too	also; too much We need some help **too**. You are walking **too** fast.	**waste**	to use carelessly We **waste** a lot of water in this house.
two	one more than one There were only **two** runners in the race.	**your**	a possessive pronoun Do you have **your** key with you?
		you're	the contraction for *you are* **You're** the favorite in the race.

5 Words Often Confused

Many words are easily confused because they have similar spellings or because they sound the same. This list includes some of these words.

accept	to receive something offered I am happy to **accept** your invitation.	**loose**	not tightly fastened The chain had become **loose**.
except	other than All the glasses **except** two were broken.	**lose**	to be unable to keep I always **lose** my pen.
affect	to have an influence on Climate **affects** the way people work.	**personal**	private She put her **personal** letters in a folder.
effect	to bring about The new law has **effected** many changes.	**personnel**	the persons employed in an organization Our **personnel** enjoy working in the new building.
clothes	items that one wears I really need new **clothes**.	**picture**	a drawn or photographic image This **picture** is very colorful.
cloths	pieces of cloth Remove the polish with these old **cloths**.	**pitcher**	(a) a baseball player who throws to a batter A new **pitcher** came into the game in the fifth inning. (b) A container from which liquid is poured. The **pitcher** of milk is cold.
desert	a dry region The **desert** is hot during the day and cold at night.		
dessert	the final part of a meal My mother served fresh fruit for **dessert**.	**precede**	to come before The band will **precede** the other marchers.
envelop	to cover A thick fog **enveloped** the beach.	**proceed**	to continue Go to the corner and then **proceed** down Maple Street.
envelope	a paper container for letters Put two stamps on this **envelope**.	**than**	used to compare My brother is taller **than** I.
later	after an expected time The train was running **later** than expected.	**then**	at that time **Then** the lights went out.
latter	closer to the end The **latter** part of the day was cloudy.		

6 Forming Plural Nouns

You have learned that a **singular noun** names one person, place, or thing. A **plural noun** names more than one person, place or thing. Check your writing to make sure you have followed these rules for spelling the plural of nouns.

- Most nouns in English add **-s** to form the plural.

  car–car**s** table–table**s** park–park**s**

- Nouns ending in s, sh, ch, or x add **-es** to form the plural.

  kiss–kiss**es** wish–wish**es** bench–bench**es** fox–fox**es**

- Nouns ending in a consonant followed by a y change the y to i and add **-es** to form the plural.

  family–famil**ies** hobby–hobb**ies** fly–fl**ies**

- Some nouns ending in f add **-s** to form the plural.

  chief–chief**s** staff–staff**s** roof–roof**s**

  Some nouns ending in f or fe change f to v and add **-s** or **-es**.

  loaf–loa**ves** knife–kni**ves** wharf–whar**ves**

- Nouns ending in a consonant followed by an o add **-es** to form the plural.

  mosquito–mosquito**es** hero–hero**es** potato–potato**es**

7 Irregular Plural Nouns

Some nouns have special plural forms. These are called irregular plurals. Some nouns have the same form for both the singular and the plural. Here is a list of nouns with irregular plurals.

Singular	Plural	Singular	Plural	Singular	Plural	Singular	Plural
child	children	louse	lice	ox	oxen	sheep	sheep
deer	deer	man	men	pants	pants	tooth	teeth
fish	fish (or fishes)	moose	moose	salmon	salmon	trout	trout
foot	feet	mouse	mice	scissors	scissors	woman	women
goose	geese						

8 Irregular Verbs

You studied irregular verbs on pages 26–28 of this book. Here is a list of almost all the irregular verbs in English. Remember, an irregular verb is one that doesn't form its past tense or past participle by adding **-d** or **-ed** to the present tense form.

Present	Present Participle	Past	Past Participle	Present	Present Participle	Past	Past Participle
bear	bearing	bore	borne	eat	eating	ate	eaten
beat	beating	beat	beaten	fall	falling	fell	fallen
begin	beginning	began	begun	fling	flinging	flung	flung
bite	biting	bit	bitten	fly	flying	flew	flown
blow	blowing	blew	blown	freeze	freezing	froze	frozen
break	breaking	broke	broken	get	getting	got	gotten
bring	bringing	brought	brought	give	giving	gave	given
burst	bursting	burst	burst	go	going	went	gone
catch	catching	caught	caught	grow	growing	grew	grown
choose	choosing	chose	chosen	know	knowing	knew	known
come	coming	came	come	lay	laying	laid	laid
creep	creeping	crept	crept	lead	leading	led	led
do	doing	did	done	lend	lending	lent	lent
draw	drawing	drew	drawn	lie	lying	lay	lain
drink	drinking	drank	drunk	lose	losing	lost	lost
drive	driving	drove	driven	ride	riding	rode	ridden

Present	Present Participle	Past	Past Participle	Present	Present Participle	Past	Past Participle
ring	ringing	rang	rung	speak	speaking	spoke	spoken
rise	rising	rose	risen	steal	stealing	stole	stolen
run	running	ran	run	sting	stinging	stung	stung
say	saying	said	said	swear	swearing	swore	sworn
see	seeing	saw	seen	swim	swimming	swam	swum
set	setting	set	set	swing	swinging	swung	swung
shake	shaking	shook	shaken	take	taking	took	taken
shine	shining	shone	shone	tear	tearing	tore	torn
sing	singing	sang	sung	throw	throwing	threw	thrown
sink	sinking	sank	sunk	wear	wearing	wore	worn
sit	sitting	sat	sat	write	writing	wrote	written

9 Four Troublesome Verbs

Two pairs of verbs in English give just about every speaker and writer trouble. These pairs of verbs are **lie** and **lay** and **set** and **sit**.

Lie and Lay

The verb **lie** means "to be at rest in a lying position." The verb's basic parts are lie, lay, (is) lying, and (have) lain. The verb **lay** means "to put or place something." The verb's basic parts are lay, laid, (is) laying, and (have) laid.

When you use these verbs, ask yourself what meaning you have in mind. Do you want to refer to someone or a thing that is in a lying position (**lie**)? Or do you want to refer to putting something down (**lay**)?

- Yesterday, Linda **lay** in bed all morning.
- I will **lie** here until I am rested.
- Sandy has **lain** in this position all day.

- I **laid** the keys on the table last night.
- All of the students have **laid** their papers on the desk.
- I will **lay** this card on top of the glass.

Sit and Set

The verb **sit** usually means "to be in an upright, sitting position." The verb's basic parts are sit, set, (is) sitting, and (have) sat. The verb **set** usually means "to put or place something." The verb's basic parts are set, set, (is) sitting, and (have) set.

To use these two verbs correctly, you must remember to use **set** when you mean to put something down. You use **sit** when you mean to sit in an upright position.

- My grandfather was **sitting** in his favorite chair.
- The boys **sat** still through the long movie.

- Clara **set** the plates on the table.
- We carefully **set** the eggs in the basket.

10 Prepositions

This list includes the most common prepositions in English.

about	at	beyond	from	past	to	until	within
above	before	but (except)	in	since	toward	up	without
across	behind	by	into	through	under	upon	
after	below	concerning	like	throughout	underneath	with	
against	beneath	down	of				
along	beside	during	off				
among	besides	except	on				
around	between	for	over				

A few groups of words are also prepositions. The most common are: because of, in spite of, on account of, and together with.

11 Contractions

This list includes the most commonly used contractions and the words they stand for.

I'm = I am	aren't = are not	they'll = they will	doesn't = does not
you're = you are	wasn't = was not	won't = will not	don't = do not
he's = he is	weren't = were not		didn't = did not
she's = she is		I've = I have	
it's = it is	I'll = I will	you've = you have	can't = cannot
we're = we are	you'll = you will	we've = we have	couldn't = could not
they're = they are	he'll = he will	they've = they have	shouldn't = should not
who's = who is	she'll = she will	hasn't = has not	wouldn't = would not
isn't = is not	we'll = we will	hadn't = had not	let's = let us
		haven't = have not	

12 Common Adverbs Not Ending in -ly

You have learned that many adverbs have the letters **-ly** at the end. Below are some commonly used adverbs that do not end in **-ly**. Some words on the list can also be used as adjectives.

We had a **late** supper. (adjective)   They arrived **late**. (adverb)

Some words can also be used as nouns.

Tomorrow will be sunny. (noun)   We will leave **tomorrow**. (adverb)

ahead	anywhere	here	nearby	often	rather	somewhere	too
almost	backward	indoors	never	once	so	then	upward
already	downward	inside	next	outdoors	soon	there	very
always	everywhere	late	now	outside	sometimes	today	yesterday
anyplace	fast	near	nowhere	quite	somewhat	tomorrow	

13 Proofreading Marks

Writers often use **proofreading marks** to correct and improve their writing. Below are some of the proofreading marks used most often. These marks can be helpful to you when you proofread your own writing.

——	take out one or more words	There was ~~was~~ a loud noise.	
ℯ	take out a letter or punctuation mark	Larry went too the beach.	
⊙	put in a period	Kay looked up⊙The sky was dark.	
⋏	put in a comma	Pat⋏ Jo, and Jim arrived.	
⋀	insert	Their⋀ wasn't too difficult. (job)	
¶	start a new paragraph	Summer was over. ¶ School began Monday.	
/	change to a small letter	Karen ran to the Park.	
≡	change to a capital letter	The leaves were lovely in october.	

Building Skills in English ■■■■■■■■■■■■■■■■■■

14 Capitalization Rules   Check the following rules for capital letters when you proofread your writing.

- Use a capital letter at the beginning of a sentence.
  When will lunch be ready?

- Use a capital letter to begin a proper noun.
  Oklahoma   Maria   Pacific Ocean

- Use a capital letter to begin a proper adjective.
  African art   Mexican city   Italian food

- Always write the word I with a capital letter.
  Janice and I jogged three miles.

- Use a capital letter to begin the first word and all important words in titles.
  Island of the Blue Dolphins   Red River Valley
  A Tale of Two Cities

- Use a capital letter to begin the first word of a direct quotation.
  Jacob asked, "What time is the picnic?"

15 Punctuation Rules   Check the following punctuation rules when you proofread your writing.

End punctuation

- Use a period at the end of a declarative or an imperative sentence.

  The room was very dark. (declarative)
  Turn on the light. (imperative)

- Use a question mark at the end of an interrogative sentence.

  Has the rain stopped?

- Use an exclamation mark at the end of an exclamatory sentence or an imperative sentence that expresses strong feeling.

  That's fantastic! (exclamatory)
  Run fast! (imperative—strong feeling)

Commas

- Use commas to separate the words in a series of three or more.

  Karen wore her yellow shirt, her jeans, and her white sweater.

- Use commas to separate words that interrupt a sentence.

  Tom, my brother, is a good swimmer.
  Who, in your opinion, is the best country singer?

- Use a comma to separate the parts of a compound sentence.

  We sat by the window for hours, and finally we saw a car.

- Use commas to separate the day and the year in dates.

  On March 8, 1986, Ben was 15 years old.

- Use commas to separate the parts of addresses or place names.

  Joe moved to 3 Oak Street, Plainview, Ohio.
  The plane landed at O'Hare Airport, Chicago.

- Use a comma to separate a direct quotation from the rest of the sentence.

  "Here's your notebook," Kim said.
  Pat asked, "What time is it?"

Quotation marks

- Use quotation marks before and after a direct quotation, or someone's exact words.

  "I walk a mile to school," Rebecca said.
  Ben shouted, "Come here!"

- In sentences that include exact words, speaker words tell who is talking. They are separated from the exact words by a comma or commas. When the speaker words come before the exact words, the comma comes before the quotation marks. (See above.) When the speaker words come after the exact words, the comma is within the quotation marks. (See above.) When speaker words come within the exact words, two commas are used. The first is inside the quotation marks. The second is outside the quotation marks.

  "I believe," said Stephen, "that it is too cold to swim."

- Use quotation marks around the titles of short stories, poems, songs, and parts of books.

  "Fog" is a poem by Carl Sandburg.
  The chorus will sing "America."

Apostrophes

- Use an apostrophe in possessive nouns.

  Jim's kite fluttered overhead.
  Listen to the horses' hooves.
  We enjoyed the children's song.

- Use an apostrophe in contractions.

  He's an hour late.
  I couldn't hear the phone ringing.

156

Colons

- Use a colon after the greeting in a business letter.

  Dear Ms. Green: Dear Madam or Sir:

  Dear Voters:

- Use a colon to separate the numbers for hours and minutes when writing the time of day.

  7:05 a.m.   6:35 p.m.   10:15 p.m.

16 Using a Dictionary

A dictionary provides information about words. You can use a dictionary to learn what words mean or how they are spelled. When you are not sure how to pronounce a word, check a dictionary.

The words in a dictionary are always in alphabetical order. Each word, along with its explanation, is called an **entry**. Two **guide words** are at the top of each dictionary page. The guide word on the left is the first word on the page. The guide word on the right is the last word on the page. The other words on the page are in alphabetical order between the two guide words.

Beside each word, the pronunciation is given. Some words have more than one pronunciation. The first listed is usually the one used most often. The word is usually divided into syllables, or units of sound. An **accent** mark (′) shows which syllable should be stressed, or said more strongly. Different marks show how to pronounce the word. A pronunciation key in the front of the dictionary tells what the marks mean. Notice the marks above the letter a below. They show the different ways in which the letter a can be pronounced.

ă pat

ā age

ä father

The marks are not the same in all dictionaries. Check the pronunciation key in your own dictionary.

The meaning of a word is called the **definition**. Some words have more than one definition. The entry might also provide other information about a word, such as its history. The part of speech, unusual plural spellings, and irregular verb forms are often included in an entry.

Study the sample dictionary items on this page.

Pronunciation   Guide words   Definition

Entry word ⎯⎯ **sand•wich** (sănd′wĭch, săn′wĭch) **1.** Two or more slices of bread with meat or other food between them. **2.** Something that looks like a sandwich, such as two slabs of material with another material between them. **3.** To put tightly between two things. **4.** To put in tight alternating layers. **5.** To fit something in on a tight schedule: *sandwich a movie between school and supper.* [After the Fourth Earl of Sandwich, for whom sandwiches were made (1718–92)]. 1, 2, *noun.* 3, 4, 5 *verb,* **sandwiched, sandwiching, sandwiches.**

Entry ⎯⎯ **Sand•wich** (sănd′wĭch, săn′wĭch) **1.** A town in eastern Kent, England. **2.** One of the oldest settlements on Cape Cod, Massachusetts (incorporated 1639). *noun.*

Sand•wich Islands (sănd′wĭch ĭ′ləndz, săn′wĭch ĭ′ləndz). The name Captain Cook gave to the Hawaiian Islands. *noun.*

sand•worm (sănd′wûrm) Any of various segmented worms, usually living on the coast in mud or sand and often used as fishing bait. *noun.*

sand•wort (sănd′wûrt, sănd′wôrt) Any of many low-growing plants with small, usually white flowers. *noun.*

sandwich | San Juan

17 Using Sources of Information

There are many different sources of information and ways to find information. The following are some of the most useful of these.

An **encyclopedia** provides articles about many different subjects. The articles are in alphabetical order. **Guide words**, at the top of a page, tell what topics are on the page. Sometimes an encyclopedia includes other articles related to a topic. These are listed at the end of an article and are called **cross-references**. Look for the words See or See also to find where to look for more information.

An encyclopedia may be one book or a set of books. One book in a set is called a **volume**. The volumes are in alphabetical order and have guide letters on the cover. These guide letters help readers choose the right volume. For example, if you were looking for information about computers, you would look in a volume with a C on the cover.

An **index** lists all of the topics in an encyclopedia. This index tells where to look for information. The index may be in the last volume in the set or in a separate volume.

An **almanac** is a book that has up-to-date facts and figures on many different topics. Almanacs are usually published every year. They include weather forecasts, information about the stars, and tide tables.

An **index** is in the back of many books that provide information. The index lists in alphabetical order the subjects in the book. Page numbers tell where information can be found.

A library **card catalogue** is a file of cards for all of the books in a library. The cards may be in file drawers or on microfilm, arranged in alphabetical order. Each card has a **call number** on it. This number tells where to find the books on the library shelves. The card gives the title of the book, the author, and the publisher. A short description of the book may also be included.

There are three kinds of cards: an **author card**, a **title card**, and a **subject card**. The author's name, last name first, is at the top of an author card. The title of the book is at the top of a title card. The subject of the book is at the top of the subject card.

18 Unlocking Word Meanings

When you are reading, you may find words that are new to you. This happens to most readers. There are a number of ways to discover the meaning of a word. You can use a dictionary, but that is not always possible. The following guidelines can help you figure out words while you are reading.

Using Clues

When you find a word you do not know, read on. You may learn what the word means by the time you finish the sentence. If not, keep on reading. Get a sense of what the whole paragraph or story is about. This can help you unlock new words.

As you read along, learn to look for **clues** to word meanings. There are different kinds of clues that readers use. These are some of the ones used most often.

- Clues that use a noun to explain

  A **whippet**, a short-haired dog, looks something like a small greyhound.

  The noun dog tells what a **whippet** is. The other words give a more complete description.

- Clues that are similar in meaning to a word

  Cleaning the fields was **arduous**. It was a very hard job.

  The word **arduous** means demanding great effort or labor. The word hard is a clue.

- Clues in words in a series

  The book had pictures of a sparrow, a robin, a thrush, and a **junco**.

  A **junco** is any of various North American birds. The words sparrow, robin, and thrush are clues.

- Clues that compare

  Sara was more **gregarious** than Martha, who liked to be alone.

  The word **gregarious** means to enjoy the company of others. The comparison to Martha, who likes to be alone, is a clue.

- Clues that state the opposite

  Jim pretended to be truthful, but everyone knew he was **deceitful**.

  The word **deceitful** means dishonest. The word truthful, the opposite of **deceitful**, is a clue.

- Clues using phrases or clauses

  When the game was over, the crowd began to **disperse**.

  The word **disperse** means to scatter in different directions. The clause When the game was over is a clue.

- Clues given by the overall mood, or feeling, in a passage

  I jumped when I heard a tapping sound. Then I looked fearfully out the window. My hand shook as it touched the cold pane. The sound of a siren only added to my **trepidation**. What was going to happen?

  The word **trepidation** means a state of alarm or dread. The feeling in the passage is a clue.